UNTIL I RETURN

UNTIL I RETURN

12 Things *Jesus* Wants
Every Believer to Know

JEFF WALLING

HOWARD
PUBLISHING CO.

Our purpose at Howard Publishing is to:

• *Increase faith* in the hearts of growing Christians

• *Inspire holiness* in the lives of believers

• *Instill hope* in the hearts of struggling people everywhere

Because He's coming again!

Until I Return © 2000 by Jeff Walling

Published by Howard Publishing Co., Inc.,
3117 North 7th Street, West Monroe, Louisiana 71291-2227

00 01 02 03 04 05 06 07 08 09   10 9 8 7 6 5 4 3 2 1

Library of Congress Cataloging-in-Publication Data
Walling, Jeff, 1957–
    Until I return : 12 things Jesus wants every believer to know / Jeff Walling.
       p. cm.
    ISBN 1-58229-094-6
       1. Bible. N.T. John XIV–XVI—Criticism, interpretation, etc. 2. Christian life—Biblical teaching. I. Title.

    BS2615.2 .W36 2000
    226.5'06—dc21

                                                            99-058939

Managing editor, Philis Boultinghouse
Manuscript editors, Amanda and Stephen Sorenson
Interior design by Stephanie Denney

Dedication

To my spiritual family, The Providence Road Church of Christ, whose elders, staff, and members keep me going.

To my ever patient physical family, who gave up time with Daddy so this work could be finished. Cathryn, Taylor, Riley, and Spencer can be found between every line.

To Kent Massey, my friend and coworker, who spurred me on in this work with a selfless vigor and a Christlike spirit. "You are the best, man!"

And to Christ, the one whose words started it all and whose return we all await. Come quickly, Lord Jesus!

CONTENTS

SETTING THE TABLE

"I'm leaving."

Jesus' words hung in the stunned silence of the dining room. Moments earlier, it had been filled with animated conversation, stories, and laughter—just what you would expect in a room full of good friends. The table was still littered with glasses of wine and scraps of bread. The platter of meat sat ready to be picked over one last time. But in an instant, all thoughts of the meal were forgotten. Those two little words stopped everything.

"I'm leaving."

Didn't they know that this day was coming? Hadn't Jesus taught them from the start that a time would come when they would need to carry on without him? Hadn't he prepared them by his example, prepped them with his teaching, and armed them with his courage?

Yes, he had. But despite his warnings and predictions, they sat in stunned disbelief. Like deer caught in the headlights, they gazed at him with slack jaws and wide eyes, amazed at the news.

They should have known that this was to be no ordinary meal. They should have known from the moment he had started washing their feet with his own hands, from the way he had blessed the cup of wine and the bread, from the deeply pensive look in his eyes. They should have known...but they didn't. Now they listened to these words as if they were hearing them for the first time.

"I'm leaving."

When it seemed the disciples would make no response, Jesus started to speak of other things that he wanted them to know. After all, the time was growing short. "A new command I give you," he began (John 13:34).

But they weren't ready for a new topic. Those two other words held them tightly. When their panic finally found its tongue, they pleaded like frightened children: "What? You're leaving?... Where are you going?... We don't understand!"

"Take me with you. I want to go too!" a bold one said.

Yes, there's the answer! they may have thought. *If you're going, we'll all go. There is no need to leave anyone behind. It'll be a wonderful trip. We can make sandwiches and pack a lunch. And when we're through, we can all come back home and share a glass of wine while we relive the memories. Hey, we could even get some souvenirs to put on the mantel!*

If they had known the destination of Jesus' journey, however, they would have retracted the idea in a heartbeat. But he quickly cut off any speculation about accompanying him by adding, "Where I am going, you cannot follow now" (John 13:36). The news was getting worse, not better. Not only was he leaving, but they weren't invited. At least not now.

One day they would all go on that journey. Peter would go soon. So would Thomas, Matthew, and James. Like the millions of believers who would follow them, the disciples would walk through the valley of the shadow of death clinging to the unseen hand of their Lord. Although some of them would die for their convictions, most would not face a cross. Some would even breathe their last breaths in peace, encircled by friends.

But that journey was in the unseen future. Their current problem was here and now. It was a pressing question for which they had no answer.

> How would they make it
> without Jesus by their side?

That question has challenged every believer since Jesus of Nazareth went to Calvary. It grows out of the strange paradox of our faith: Our Lord is with us, yet he is away from us. From the instant we are born again until the moment we leave this world, we exist in an "in-between" time—a no-man's land of waiting to be with the one we adore. We have said good-bye to a life of human aims but not yet said hello to eternity in a divine place. Yes, Christ's "presence" may be real enough to the heart, but our eyes long to see him. Our hands long to join Thomas's in touching the wounds he received on our behalf. We desire to be "with the Lord," as Paul wrote to the Philippians. But for now, we must wait for his return.

So we find ourselves asking the disciples' question: "How do we live while we wait?"

With the wisdom and love that only the Master can possess, Jesus began to share with his frightened followers the words they would need until he returned. These words would fill the void the other two words had created. These words would guide and direct the disciples, soothe and assure them. These words would enable them to live, for a while, without him by their side.

These precious words are found uniquely in the Gospel of John. Rather than focusing his attention on the meal itself, as the other writers did, John chose to focus on the words Jesus spoke.

Words of comfort.

Words of warning.

Words of encouragement.

Words of caution.

During the remainder of that wonderful evening before that awful night had fully begun, Jesus gave his disciples just the words they would need to face the trials of his absence. Like a divine parent preparing for a trip across the galaxy, he sat his children down at what would be their last meal together and calmed their fears with his words. Word by word, phrase by phrase, he gave them the spiritual nourishment they would need in order to stay healthy as they made their journey home. The meal he offered consisted of simple words any child could recite. They were words he wanted every believer to know: Don't fear. Stay close. Trust me. But they were—

and are—powerful words that no demon can conquer, no unbeliever can comprehend.

So come, sit at the table with our Lord. Push the plate aside and listen. Drink deeply and fill your heart with the words he offers. You won't need a knife or fork to digest this meal—just an open heart and a willing ear. Come, sit close by his side while he speaks, and listen to the life-giving words we all need until he returns.

SECTION ONE
WORDS OF COMFORT

My brother-in-law is afraid of flying, but he will deny it till his dying day: "I just don't like being cooped up in an oversized soup can for hours!" He'll blame his dislike on the uncomfortable airplane seats or the bad food, but the dirty truth is *he's scared to get on a plane.*

So what are you afraid of?

Being alone in the dark or being left alone by your spouse? Getting lost in woods or getting pancreatic cancer? The thing under your bed or the thing you did last summer?

You see, whatever we fear rules us. It takes control of our lives. Jesus knew that fear would be the reaction of his followers when he told them that he would be leaving. So the first three things he wants every believer to know have to do with fear and how to conquer it.

> "Don't be afraid."
> "Don't stop trusting."
> "You're not alone."

The words are simple enough, but the power within them is limitless. There is enough muscle in those words to push fear right out of a human heart. There is sufficient power in those truths to cure the crippling effects fear leaves in its victims' lives. And they were spoken by a savior strong enough to make them work in your life today.

Why, they might even get my brother-in-law on a plane. Let's look at them together and see if you agree.

$\mathcal{D}$o not let your hearts be troubled. Trust in God; trust also in me. In my Father's house are many rooms; if it were not so, I would have told you. I am going there to prepare a place for you. And if I go and prepare a place for you, I will come back and take you to be with me that you also may be where I am. You know the way to the place where I am going.

John 14:1–4

1

DON'T BE AFRAID

"You have *heart trouble.*"

Those words can strike fear into the hardiest soul, so when a young and coldly efficient cardiologist spoke them to my eighty-year-old mother, you can be sure that they got my attention.

It happened a few years ago when a ten-day visit from Mom turned into a major crisis. She fell at our home and broke her right hip and wrist. The wrist was handled with a simple cast, but the hip required surgery. Flying her home to California for the procedure was not an option, and the local doctors wanted a complete assessment of her health before they would operate. So my mother, a very private senior citizen who went to see her family doctor only under threat of death, had strangers by the dozens prying into every facet of her physical condition. She was not a happy camper.

I, however, was pleased with their thoroughness and asked one patient doctor plenty of questions.

"Is this a new condition?"

"Was it caused by the fall?"

"What kind of heart trouble are we talking about?"

"No, it's not connected to her fall," he assured me. "It's called *arrhythmia*. She has an irregular heartbeat."

"Oh, I've had that for years," Mom interjected in her *Don't-you-think-I-knew-that-already-Mr.-Smarty-Pants?* tone of voice. "I take my heart medicine every day, and I get along just fine."

Indeed, I discovered that my mother had learned, through the years, how to live an active life despite a chronic heart condition that had dropped other folks in their tracks. She had grown so used to her heart trouble that she had learned to ignore it. The surgeon's words reminded her of the vital truth: "You may not think this is important, but ignoring it could cost you your life!"

Isn't that what Christ wanted his followers to remember as well?

As he began to teach his disciples during that final night, he wanted to ensure that their hearts not be troubled. Moreover, he did not want Christians throughout the ages to live in a state of fear that would trouble their hearts. One could say that Jesus wanted to warn all of us against heart trouble. Although no bottle of Cardizem will protect our hearts from fear, the Great Physician gave us a prescription just the same. It doesn't come in "pill form," however. It comes in "command form":

"Don't be afraid."

That's the core of the first advice Christ gave his disciples to enable them to face the time until his return. But his message was more than just "don't be afraid." He was actually saying, "Don't allow your hearts to be troubled by fear." More than just telling his followers to stop being afraid at a given moment, Jesus commanded them to take control of their feelings. For if they did not, those feelings would take control of them. Sadly, many believers have ignored this simple directive from their Lord and have lived in fear of life itself. Momentary fright is one thing, but to live every day in fear is to lose the battle of life.

And what is living with fear? It is growing accustomed to constant worry about our lives and souls. It is accepting the uneasy feeling that our salvation is not secure and our future is in question. It is a devilish détente with doubt that makes inner peace impossible.

Living with fear also means resigning control. Slowly, the fears we accept start to direct our path. It becomes easier to compensate for our fears rather than to face them. Much like learning to live with an irregular heartbeat or a dysfunctional limb, we adjust our routine to accommodate our fears and so allow them to become our unspoken master. One person I know will never see Europe or Hawaii because he refuses to fly. Another's fear of computers keeps her from enjoying the benefits of word processing and electronic mailing.

And the damage doesn't stop there. Fear can rob us of joy and bind us in panic. It messes up our minds and confounds our common sense. When we're alone and in the dark, fear whispers unthinkable terrors in our ears. Our hearts begin to race. Our minds invent visions of disaster.

CHAPTER 1

What if I get cancer?

What if my spouse leaves me?

What if my children rebel?

A vicious spiral begins, and we find ourselves riding a self-constructed slide into despair. Fear begets fear, and soon even the most irrational of concerns can leave us demoralized and immobilized.

Sound familiar? Living with fear is the kind of heart trouble from which some people never seem to recover. But compared with the spiritual impact, these emotional effects are unimportant. When fear takes control over our faith, it renders us ineffective in doing the very tasks to which our Lord has called us.

Talk to my neighbor about my faith?

—Oh no, I'd be afraid.

Confront my friends about their deceit?

—I'm afraid I just couldn't.

Stand up for my beliefs in front of others?

—I'm too afraid.

Jesus would have none of it. Looking into the frightened faces of his disciples, he gave a command—not a suggestion.

"Don't give in to fear."

But how, then, do we follow our Lord's "be fearless" order? Before we try to swallow the biblical prescription for spiritual arrhythmia, we need a moment to digest the history of mankind's first real enemy and learn three important facts about fear.

1. $\mathcal{F}$ear Has Always Been Connected to Sin

Fear started in the beautiful garden God designed for humankind, his premier creation. The Genesis account describes the garden as an ideal environment. Everything humankind needed was within reach. From the daylight necessary to eat and exercise to the darkness that prompted rest and sleep, the world was a perfect place. In fact, the way the world conforms to our human needs is one of the great testimonies to man's primacy and God's ingenuity.

Within that original, optimal habitat, man knew no fear. The word *fear* is not even mentioned in Scripture prior to the first sin. Why? There was no *cause* for fear. The animals were in subjection to man, and the gardens were without weeds. Disease and decomposition were unknown. Humankind lived in submission to God and in perfect harmony with creation, which makes the temptation Satan offered all the more astounding.

Satan had the gall to suggest to a woman who lived in an ideal environment with the only man on earth as her mate and the Lord of creation as her friend that he could offer her more.

Think about it: Within the garden, Eve possessed all of the blessings God had provided in his will: family, love, peace, assurance, and joy. And the tempter suggested that one little step beyond the boundary of God's will would bring inconceivable delights. It sounded interesting. It sounded inviting. It sounded like just what Eve needed after a tough week. So she looked both ways before crossing God's line and then took one tiny step, expecting ecstasy.

How wrong she was. The product was nothing like the advertisement. Instead of stepping into utopia, she was run over by a Mack truck with a four-letter license plate: FEAR. And all humanity has been stepping over that line ever since.

You look over your shoulder before you step into the topless bar.

You scan the block for familiar cars before you stop at your "friend's" house.

You get uncomfortably nervous when discussions of integrity and hypocrisy get too close to home.

Fear seems like a reasonable choice when you're looking through guilt-colored glasses. Sin opens the door, and fear enters on the heels of its twin demon, guilt. They pull up seats at the table and make themselves right at home. And they will shape your life just as they drove Adam and Eve to hide in the bushes.

What a neat, nasty system. Sin destroys the foundation of our confidence by eroding our relationship with God and replacing it with fear. It leaves us feeling dirty, scared, and unsure of our salvation. *Can God forgive me of this…again?* we wonder. Although we may not like it, we learn to live with the fear because it came prepackaged with the deceit. No assembly was necessary.

But how does fear take control so quickly? Wherein is its power?

2. The Power of Fear Is a Matter of Focus

When Adam and Eve realized the gravity of their mistake, they instinctively responded in fear. They tried to cover their bodies and their tracks. They foolishly hid from the Lord. When questioned, Adam confessed:

"I was afraid because I was naked; so I hid" (Genesis 3:10).

Where had the peace of mind that must have existed in paradise gone? Adam and Eve's peace of mind vanished when the *focus* of their attention shifted from God's power to their weakness. Fear caused them to forget about the loving way God had provided for them and the gracious way he had sustained them. They instantly developed a kind of fear-driven tunnel vision that allowed them to see nothing but an oncoming train.

Doesn't fear work the same way with us?

Consider the amazing way everything else vanishes when fear grabs our attention. Remember the last time you screamed out loud when someone tapped you on the shoulder unexpectedly? There you stood in the safety of your own kitchen when suddenly you were scared out of your wits...and you were wearing the cup of coffee you had been about to drink! When fear seizes the controls, nothing else matters.

From a spiritual perspective, the result of fear is no different. We can literally be struck deaf and blind with fear. We become unable to hear the words of peace the Holy Spirit brings or the comforting truths the Father offers in his Word. Most important, we lose sight of God. Like Peter as he walked on the storm-tossed water toward Jesus, we take one look at the waves, and fear takes control. We lose our focus, and we're sunk—literally and spiritually.

That same loss of proper focus also inhibits our growth in Christ. When God challenges us to move beyond our comfort zones or to take a step in faith, fear isn't far away. We may be bold about singing out in worship or discussing God with friends of like mind, but change the setting, and fear will curb our freedom quickly enough. How? Fear simply refocuses our eyes on the opposition. It directs our attention to the rejection we might suffer. Presto! We're paralyzed by panic.

Between the guilt-centered power of sin and the distracting ability of panic, fear looks unbeatable. But even fear has its weakness. It has no power unless we are *looking* in the *direction* it prescribes. As long as fear holds the telescope, we'll keep staring at the pending disaster or anticipated punishment. That's why it takes real discipline to stay scared. You have to keep focusing on the object of your fear. When you change your focus, the fear vanishes.

Watch construction workers on a high-rise building, for example. Focused on their goal, they jump with seeming abandon from one girder to the next at heights that would paralyze most of us. But let one of them misstep and tumble thirty stories, and watch the rest of the crowd. Even the most jaded will take a little more time crossing the job site as fear comes roaring back with a vengeance, demanding to be noticed.

In a similar way, Jesus turns the power of fear on its head by restoring our focus. He reminds us that if our eyes are fixed by faith on God and his nature rather than being directed by fear, there is no room for anxiety. It is as though Christ challenges you and me to name our greatest fear. Is it cancer? Loneliness? Bankruptcy? Death? No matter what the fear, it evaporates when the eyes of our hearts are fixed on the Lord. His presence dismisses dread. His touch drives out terror. His unending power—matched only by his unending love—simply leaves no room for fear...at least not the heart-troubling kind.

But there is one fear Christ would never have us lose.

3. *C*onquering Fear Is a Matter of Choice

Jesus' command to "fear not" needs to be viewed in light of another kind of fear, a healthy one that the Bible calls the "fear of the Lord." Jesus never intended for his followers to lose this proper respect for God, but he did intend for them to lose their fear of everything else. He chastised the disciples for worrying about food and clothes, but he never said that all fear was to be avoided. What he did demand was that his followers learn what to fear. Or better still, *whom* to fear: "I tell you, my friends, do not be afraid of those who kill the body and after that can do no more. But I will show you whom you should fear: Fear him who, after the killing of the body, has power to throw you into hell. Yes, I tell you, fear him" (Luke 12:4–5).

Throughout the Bible, God's presence has caused fear in people, yet God's presence also banishes fear in people. Consider these passages from David and Isaiah:

> Though I walk through the valley of the shadow of death, I will fear no evil. (Psalm 23:4)

> Surely God is my salvation; I will trust and not be afraid. (Isaiah 12:2)

Compare those with this one:

> The fear of the LORD is the beginning of knowledge.
> (Proverbs 1:7)

The key to keeping our hearts from being troubled is choosing whom to fear! Faith is actually the choice to fear God only. Put another way, it is deciding between the greater of two fears. My father taught me this principle years ago in a chicken coop.

Although our family lived in the city, Dad made sure we didn't miss out on the wonders of farm life. He planted a garden in the tiny spot of land we had behind our house to show us what green peas looked like before they ended up on our table. And he brought home three little chicks.

Dad put some chicken wire across a dog run at the side of the house and built a small roost. Soon my siblings and I learned to feed and water the chickens; we even gathered eggs.

Well, we gathered at least one egg. Apparently, two of the little chicks were male. Within a few weeks, one found its way onto a platter at Sunday lunch. The trauma that event caused my younger sister lingers to this day: She shudders at the very mention of KFC. The other rooster was allowed to live, and he literally ruled the roost. Dad decided to let some of the eggs hatch, and soon, more little chicks were scampering everywhere. The rooster seemed to take great pride in all of this, but he also became more protective of his territory.

One day, as I carried a fresh pan of water into the pen to set out for the new chicks, that rooster *attacked* me. My father later told me that "flogged" was the appropriate term, but semantic distinctions were the least of my concerns when the rooster ran at me with his wings flapping wildly. He came within inches of my tennis shoes, then he backed up and ruffled his feathers defiantly. Startled, and wrongly assuming he was just playing with me, I chose to ignore him and bent down to place the pan close to the chickens' food trough.

Seizing the opportunity, the rooster struck. He flapped his wings enough to get himself momentarily airborne! This was shock enough, but then he turned his feet up with the heels facing me. I hadn't noticed until that moment how sharp the little spurs on the back of his feet were—sharp enough to do some serious gouging of my tender flesh, not to mention what they might do to my twenty-twenty vision!

With a scream that sounded more like it came from my sister than from me, I threw the water pan into the air and bolted for the back door of the house. I had left the chicken pen gate unlatched, but I had escaped alive! Dad met me as I lunged into the back pantry, slamming and locking the door behind me.

"What happened to you?" he said, pointing to my soaked shirt and ashen face.

"The rooster tried to kill me!" I held back the tears fairly well as I detailed the attack.

But I lost it when Dad shook his head and gave me this suicide mission: "Go back out there. Refill that pan, relatch the gate, and show that rooster who's boss."

That's when I began to cry. I knew who the boss was, and I had no interest in challenging his domain. I argued that I could get hurt, that the chickens could drink the water on the ground, and finally that the rooster was really my father's problem because he had bought him in the first place! But no amount of debate or protest softened my father's resolve. He just stuffed a rolled-up newspaper into my hand, grabbed me by the arm, and headed outside with me. When I resisted, struggling to remain in the safety of the house, he gave me one of his looks that said silently but clearly, "If you don't get going right now, you are going to get it."

Knowing full well what "it" was and how long my seat would sting if I got "it," I had a crucial decision to make: Would I rather face the wrath of my father or take the chance on losing my life in hand-to-feathers combat with an angry chicken? The choice was a no-brainer. The rooster was a frightening opponent, but he was nothing compared to my dad. I chose to face my fear in the chicken pen by submitting to my fear and respect for my father.

As believers in Christ, we must make the same choice. While we await the return of our Lord, fears will fly in our face, threatening to deter us from our tasks.

The fear of hurting feelings may try to stop us
from disciplining our children.

The fear of straining relationships might seek to
keep us from sharing our faith in Jesus with a friend.

The fear of being vulnerable could hamstring us
when we move to confess our faults or admit a wrong.

But when compared to facing the wrath of the God who calls you and me to complete those tasks, those other fears are downright minuscule. They don't deserve to be described with the same word. Indeed, once we choose to fear the Lord, there is nothing else of consequence left to fear! With him as our protector, redeemer, and Lord, what can truly frighten us?

And as for that rooster? Well, let's just say that he turned out to be rather tender, sweet, and great with mashed potatoes and gravy.

Thomas said to him, "Lord, we don't know where you are going, so how can we know the way?"

Jesus answered, "I am the way and the truth and the life. No one comes to the Father except through me. If you really knew me, you would know my Father as well. From now on, you do know him and have seen him."

Philip said, "Lord, show us the Father and that will be enough for us."

Jesus answered, "Don't you know me, Philip, even after I have been among you such a long time? Anyone who has seen me has seen the Father. How can you say, 'Show us the Father'?... I tell you the truth, anyone who has faith in me will do what I have been doing. He will do even greater things than these, because I am going to the Father. And I will do whatever you ask in my name, so that the Son may bring glory to the Father."

John 14:5–13

2
DON'T STOP TRUSTING

My youngest son stood, his toes hanging over the edge of the pool, and peered down at the water. His gaze wasn't tough to translate. It clearly said, "No way!"

We had been working up to this moment all summer, and I had hoped to capture it for our family video collection. In my mind, the scene was called "Spencer Jumps into the Pool," and it had gone without a hitch. I could narrate the scene in my sleep. *The confident and trustworthy father* (that's me) *has carefully accustomed his young son* (that would be Spencer) *to the water. With strong arms at the ready, the father motions for the boy to jump in and trust his dad to keep him afloat. The son, with complete confidence, leaps into the water and into the arms of his trustworthy dad while onlookers marvel at the power-ful bond of love and trust between father and son.*

But Spencer wasn't leaping.

He wasn't jumping.

He wasn't even moving.

Moreover, I was aware that some friends who had been swimming and playing with their kids had stopped to watch this battle of the wills. I smiled, opened my arms wide, and quietly begged my son to take the plunge. "Come on, Spence. I'm right here. You can do it for Daddy. Pleeeease?" But no amount of coaxing would convince him to leave the security of terra firma by his own choice.

My son was not yet three, but he had already learned one of life's simplest lessons: You can't always trust the guy who says, "Jump. I'll catch you!" As he grew up, he would encounter dozens of ways to express that doubt in others.

"I'll believe it when I see it."

"Don't count your chickens until…"

"When they say, 'The check is in the mail'…"

"Show me the money!"

And in this life there are good reasons for all the clichés. Getting scammed in business and duped in relationships are common occurrences. For many people, *trust* and *integrity* are words fit only for Hallmark cards. They believe that the only way to be sure of anything is to get it in writing—and then have your lawyer ready to defend every line of the contract.

So how does a person live in a world in which disbelief is standard operating procedure? You do just what Spencer did: You doubt, and you hold out for familiar ground. In fact, most of us become experts at doubting. We question every advertisement and quiz every salesperson. We scan the fine print looking for the loophole we know must be there. We cruise the supermarket receipt just to make sure we weren't charged twice for the bananas. Cynicism and skepticism become second nature, and the bumper sticker on the family car may as well read, "Trust no one."

But then we drive the car to church on Sunday—bumper sticker and all—where we hear the preacher tell us to place our trust...

> In a God we can't prove
>> Who promises to take us to a heaven we can't see
>>> Because a Savior we haven't met
>>>> Died for the sins we can't get rid of.

Right! It seems as if God is blithely telling us, "Jump in. The water's fine!" Who could place their trust so freely in something so intangible? Yet every Sunday we sing with gusto about how we trust in him and are ready to take any leap of faith he requests.

Admittedly, there are times when we truly feel free of doubt and stand firm in our convictions. On those days, it is no trouble to obey the command Jesus gave to his disciples during the Last Supper: "Trust in God; trust also in me" (John 14:1). Those are the victory days when doing what's right comes easy. They are the times when we calmly choose to tell the truth or take an unpopular but godly stand. We know it might cost us, but we are confident that the strong arms of our Father will catch us.

I'm convinced that every believer starts out with lots of victory days. Those days are sweet, but often fleeting. While we wait for

Jesus' return, our confidence often erodes. Then the other days come: the days when answers to prayer get lost in the mail, when faith in Jesus feels so flimsy compared to the rough reality of death or disease. These are the times when God seems distant at best and nonexistent at worst. Christians don't like to talk about these dark days when the winds of doubt blow across the landscape of faith. It is on these days that the truly tough questions are unearthed.

What do I do with these nagging doubts about you?
How can I know you will be there for me?
Why should I trust you, Jesus?

I believe that any Christian who claims to have never wrestled with these doubts needs to reread the commandment about lying. And anyone who believes that a person simply "grows out of doubting" as he or she matures in Christ has a sad surprise ahead. As long as the mind is active, doubts never disappear. Doubts are the dumbbells of faith that must be lifted and lowered countless times in order to build the muscles of true belief.

But facing doubt and examining one's core beliefs is tough work, and some of us would rather develop a mental détente with doubt. We strike an agreement between our brains and our hearts that we will not ask such questions, and we make a pact to muzzle or ignore anyone who does. We even go so far as to suggest that faith in Jesus is a decision a person makes one day and never questions again.

But those of us who wrestle with doubt can take heart in our Lord's message to his disciples that final night. He knew that the battle for their faith would grow more difficult when he was no longer with them in the flesh. Rather than ignoring the issue, he put those frightful questions on the table. He invited the disciples to ask themselves again, *Do I trust this man?*

Jesus wanted every believer to know that the tough questions of faith must be asked over and over again. While choosing to trust Christ may happen in one day, reaffirming that trust must happen every day. So let's take a look at some of these tough questions. Let's check the waters of our faith with the minds God has given us, using the standard questions we all learned in eighth-grade English class: Who? What? When? Where? Why?

Who Did Jesus Claim to Be?

I called a radio talk show for the first time in my life a few weeks ago. I had been driving back from a late appointment and was listening to the city's favorite "all-talk" station. The host was ranting about a million-dollar, statewide Christian media campaign that used billboards and television ads with this simple message: "Jesus is the power to change." The host took exception to one word: *the.* "How can anyone with half a brain," he sneered, "suggest that there is only one way to live your life, that there is only one person through whom all people must make their peace with God?" As he blew away one defensive Christian caller after another, I became angrier and angrier. When I reached my house, I decided to call the guy. After all, the chances of my getting on the show were probably nil, I thought. But within thirty seconds of being put on hold, I heard, "And let's hear what Jeff from Charlotte has to say."

My brain went blank for a frightening second.

"Jeff, are you there?"

"Uh, yeah.... Thanks for taking my call," I mumbled on autopilot. I couldn't believe I was actually on the air.

"Well, what's your comment?"

This was my shot. But how could I defend the notion that there is only one way to have true life? How can a believer explain away freedom of choice, a concept that is so esteemed in our culture and heritage that no one even argues about it anymore? We are free to live where we want, work where we want, eat what we want, and pick the car we want. So why can't we choose any religion we want? Isn't one religion just as good as another? No! So I gave it my best.

"What bothers me, Mike, is that you seem so utterly convinced that there could not possibly be one right way to live. Isn't that the same narrow-mindedness that you accuse Christians of? Don't you admit that it is *possible* that there is one right way to live? Don't you have to agree that Jesus *might* be just who he said he was: God on earth?"

"Well, sure, the possibility exists," Mike admitted, "but it's just that. It's a possibility, and some of his claims are downright outlandish! Wouldn't you agree?"

In one sense, that talk-show host was right. The claims of Jesus are outlandish at first glance, and even at a second or third glance. Listen to his claims: "I am *the* way and *the* truth and *the* life" (John 14:6). There is nothing petty in those statements. Jesus strides onto the stage of history and proclaims himself to be not only the star performer but the playwright as well. He emphatically claims that

He is *the* one way, and he does it in a world that hates one-way streets:

No one comes to the Father except through *me*. (John 14:6)

Whoever disowns *me* before men, I will disown him before my Father in heaven. (Matthew 10:33)

All authority in heaven and on earth has been given to *me*. (Matthew 28:18)

Have you ever felt the need to apologize for Christ's claims? I mean, when you stare at them on the page, they seem almost unbelievable. The amazing breadth of Christ's claims has even caused some believers, cowed by the jeers of a skeptical crowd, to try to soften the outlandish nature of those claims. "There could be other ways to heaven, but we certainly believe that Jesus is one," they whimper. "Jesus is the answer for me. You have to find yours," they timidly suggest.

But the path of appeasement leads only to more trouble. For if you swallow the pill of pluralism, some of Christ's words will stick in your throat: "If you do not believe that I am the one I claim to be, you will indeed *die in your sins*" (John 8:24). Jesus just didn't leave much wiggle room.

Even so, the logic of accommodation through mitigation has had powerful proponents. Great theologians and scholars have chosen to deny some miracles of Christ. They excise from the Bible any claims or stories that don't fit their logical mind-set. Whenever we do this, however, we don't end up with Jesus. We end up with a nice guy who taught nice things and then died on a cross. There is no resurrection—it's too unexplainable. There is no ascension—it's too unbelievable. The result is *Jesus Lite:* great teachings—less divinity.

But God won't drink such a concoction, and neither should we. Jesus doesn't need us to dress him up in the "right" clothes so we can introduce him to our friends. He prefers to confront all men as he is—the unique Jesus, the unexplainable Christ, the one who must be believed. Jesus invites us to trust him. Then he allows us to examine exhaustively the evidence for that trust.

What Did Jesus Do to Prove His Claims?

Evidence is the stuff of courtrooms and trials. No lawyer, at least not a good one, says to the jury, "Just believe me." Instead, a good lawyer presents the jury with the facts of the case and asks the jurors to decide based on that evidence. And that is what Jesus did when he said to Thomas: "Reach out your hand and put it into my side" (John 20:27).

Regrettably, the courtroom is not the model used in most religious discussions. Often the person who shouts the loudest is proclaimed the winner. Even worse, many Christians mistakenly believe they cannot win the battle for faith on the field of facts. They fear that the story of Jesus will melt like spun sugar if it is exposed to the heat of factual inquiry. But nothing could be farther from the truth. The evidence in Jesus' defense is substantial.

Consider for a moment the case of noted Christian author and former skeptic Josh McDowell. After years of mocking the Christian faith, as a bright college student, Josh agreed to a factual debate. He set out to research the claims of Christ and prove them wrong. Unfortunately for his atheistic cohorts, his hours of study into the archaeological and historical background of the Scriptures yielded an embarrassing finding. Given the evidence, the most reasonable and logical conclusion was that Jesus is God's Son.

In his popular description of the process, *Evidence That Demands a Verdict,* McDowell writes that there is more factual, historic substantiation for the existence of Jesus than for the existence of Plato and Socrates put together. Yet no one questions the existence of these philosophical giants of history. McDowell further suggests that Christ's resurrection is the single greatest evidence for the trustworthiness of Christ's claims. Once a person admits that Jesus came back from the dead, the rest of his miracles and teachings are accepted without question.

The apostle Paul came to this same conclusion: "If there is no resurrection of the dead, then not even Christ has been raised. And if Christ has not been raised, our preaching is useless and so is your faith" (1 Corinthians 15:13–14). He knew that all the claims of Jesus hinge on the reality of his death, burial, and resurrection. Without the resurrection, we are awash in fuzzy precepts and theoretical propositions. The empty tomb offers firsthand testimony: "Jesus was here, and then he rose." When the winds of doubt blow on your faith concerning Jesus' resurrection, ask yourself this question: "If he wasn't resurrected, what happened? If the tomb is empty, where did he go?"

Nonbelievers through the years have concocted some pretty wild explanations for the empty tomb. One widely promoted theory suggests that Jesus' body was stolen from the grave. Although it sounds plausible, this theory doesn't stand up to logical cross-examination. Consider the facts: The tomb was guarded by a Roman guard unit that typically consisted of four to sixteen men who had been trained since age twelve for one task: to guard six square feet of ground against an entire oncoming army. Any Roman soldier found asleep on duty was subject to immediate execution. How's that for motivation to stay awake and alert?

So, who was capable of ambushing the four to sixteen highly trained and motivated Roman brutes guarding the tomb of Jesus and making off with his body? Skeptics point the finger of suspicion at the apostles as the most likely body snatchers. Really? Did that ragtag band of doubting tax collectors and fishermen, who were fighting amongst themselves for position only hours before Jesus was taken, suddenly coalesce into an elite band of nocturnal commandos? Did they sneak up on the Roman guards and beat them with mackerels and moneybags, spirit away the body of Jesus, and then lie about the whole encounter even as they were martyred? I don't think so.

And why would they have stolen Jesus' body? For riches? For property? For power? No, if the apostles stole Jesus' body, they perpetrated the greatest hoax in history so that they could become penniless paupers and fugitives from the law who would die horrific deaths by torture, beheading, and imprisonment.

And that's just *one* of the strange theories that try to explain Jesus' resurrection. Another theory suggests that he just swooned on the cross and—after three days without food, water, or much fresh air— got well! Still another claims that the soldiers and apostles who discovered that Jesus' body was missing made the simple error of going into the wrong tomb. That's right—just three days after they buried the most famous man of his time, they forgot where they put him!

Don't feel bad if you have a hard time reading these theories with a straight face. I am constantly amazed by the number of folks who buy these kinds of explanations and then accuse Christians of stepping out in blind faith. Belief in any of these theories requires a greater suspension of logic than belief in the simplest explanation— Jesus rose.

Thousands of skeptics and doubters throughout the centuries have come to the same conclusion that Josh McDowell did: Jesus, God's Son, did come back from the dead. And millions of Christians have reviewed the evidence for faith in our risen Lord countless times when the wait for his return has worn their trust thin. But the evidence for our faith is not all in the ancient past. We can test our trust in Jesus by using our personal lives as well.

When Has Jesus Let Us Down?

Is Jesus trustworthy? That's the ultimate credibility question. It encompasses judging both character and integrity. Trustworthiness is the estimate of truthfulness yet to be witnessed in trials yet to be faced, but on what can we base our decisions to trust anybody?

Typically, we base decisions of trustworthiness on a track record.

Judging trustworthiness is predicting future honesty based on past performance, such as, "He has never lied to me" or "She has always been faithful." Although past honesty is no guarantee of future trustworthiness, it's the best gauge we have.

So let's apply it to Jesus. In what ways has he been trustworthy in his promises? Subjectivity is unavoidable in answering this question because each of us can only testify to our own experience, but listen to the long line of witnesses who will gladly testify to the faithful love of Christ:

> Christ loves each of us as if there were only one of us.
> —Saint Augustine of Hippo (354–430)

> Before the mountains were brought forth, and long ere the light flashed through the sky, God loved his chosen creatures.
> —Charles Haddon Spurgeon (1834–1892)

> Give yourself up with joy to a loving confidence in God and have courage to believe firmly that God's action toward you is a masterpiece of partiality and love.
> —Abbe Henri de Tourville (1842–1903)

> Christ's love is an incomprehensibly vast, bottomless, shore-less sea before which we kneel in joyful silence and from which the loftiest eloquence retreats confused and abashed.
> —A. W. Tozer (1897–1963)

And let me add one more, less-famous name to the list: mine.

Jesus' love has always been trustworthy. Every time he has warned that an action would be harmful to me by calling it sin, he has been right. Every time his words have counseled me toward a tougher but more noble choice, his advice has been sound. Through more than a quarter of a century of testing his path, I have discovered time and again that his way was the best way, his choices the best choices.

—Jeff Walling (1957–)

What about you? When you have moments of doubt and frustration as you await the King's return, look seriously at your walk with Jesus. Has he ever been wrong? Has his Word ever steered you down a dead-end street or made you take a wrong turn? Through times of difficulty and days of ease, Jesus remains an advisor whose credibility has no parallel. His word is as good as gold…even better!

But there remain two final questions before the witness can be excused.

Where Else Could We Turn?

When doubts plague the Christian's heart, they have a strange way of turning the choice of faith into a binary equation: Choose to believe in Jesus or choose not to believe in Jesus. Although this view of our choices is true, it is hardly complete. There are only two perspectives, but there is also the matter of alternatives. And they matter a lot!

Suppose you are struggling with your faith in Christ and one day choose not to believe in Jesus. Don't let Satan convince you that such a choice ends your problems or closes the debate. In fact, that choice brings you to the worst part of the debate, which the first followers of Christ faced in John 6. Jesus had laid out some especially hard teaching, and some of his followers chose to follow him no more. As the deserters walked away, the faces of the remaining disciples must have betrayed their own inner struggles. Jesus, as recorded in John 6:67–69, didn't miss the chance to make them face the alternative: "'You do not want to leave too, do you?' Jesus asked the Twelve. Simon Peter answered him, 'Lord, to whom shall we go? You have the words of eternal life. We believe and know that you are the Holy One of God.'"

There it is! If you choose not to follow Jesus, where will you turn? What is your alternative? It's one thing to argue against Christ's divinity, but what argument can be marshaled in support of any other leader's divinity? Other leaders and teachers have come and gone, but none has had the impact or the power of Jesus. Other spiritual guides have sought to make their marks and establish their followings, but no others have caused the whole world to set its calendar by their birthdays.

If you choose to follow no one and believe only in yourself, the prospects are even dimmer. No one knows our own faults and shortcomings like we do. A long, hard look in the mirror will cure most of us from the notion that we can make it on our own. Between the frailty of our bodies and the limitations of our minds, we humans have ample proof that we are not gods. That's why mankind has long believed that there has to be someone greater, someone wiser to whom we can turn. That's why Peter's words are so direct and pointed. If we choose not to follow Jesus, where can we turn?

When all the other alternatives have proved less than desirable, we arrive at last at our final question.

Why Not Trust Jesus?

As Jesus looked into the eyes of his weary disciples during that night long ago, did he know how long the world would have to wait for his return? The disciples would face their doubts for the next three days following his death, but then glorious proof would come in the form of the resurrected Christ. The disciples needed Jesus' words to get them through the week, but what about the rest of us? We need Jesus' words to get us through life! Our war with doubt has already lasted nearly two thousand years, and only God knows how many more years we must wait. Yet Jesus offers us the same invitation to confidence that he offered to his first disciples:

"Trust me."

And Jesus is always willing for us to put him to the test.

So after asking who, what, when, and where, we are left with a simple *why:* Why not trust Jesus? It may seem trivial, but our greatest gift lies in this question. Although the evidence may be overwhelming and the alternatives unsavory, our God gives us the right to choose. We don't have to follow Jesus. We are free to give in to doubt and cynicism and go our own way. Or we can leap out in faith into his waiting and trustworthy arms.

Over the last two thousand years, Jesus has proven himself trustworthy in the lives of millions. In sickness and in health, in good times and in need, he has been faithful. That is why so many people around the world have found themselves asking, "Why not trust Jesus?"

And to that question, they find no good answer.

Whoever has my commands and obeys them, he is the one who loves me. He who loves me will be loved by my Father, and I too will love him and show myself to him.

All this I have spoken while still with you. But the Counselor, the Holy Spirit, whom the Father will send in my name, will teach you all things and will remind you of everything I have said to you.

John 14:21, 25–26

3

YOU ARE NOT ALONE

The story of Senator John McCain is one every American should know. It comes from the frightening and confusing days of the Vietnam War and centers on one room, a cell at the POW compound dubbed the "Hanoi Hilton." There McCain, then a lieutenant in the U.S. Marines, lived for more than five years. During much of his imprisonment, he endured solitary confinement. He was allowed little or no contact with other prisoners and was forced to spend his days accompanied only by his thoughts.

McCain later said that he maintained his sanity during that ordeal by devising tricks to prove to himself that he was not truly alone. He and the other prisoners developed a communication system that consisted of tapping on the walls of their cells in a crude form of Morse code. Using this slow and difficult process, they could send short messages back and forth. Often these messages consisted of just two words: *Stay strong.* Were it not for this tenuous contact with his fellow prisoners, McCain says that loneliness would have destroyed him.

McCain's conclusion should come as no surprise. Loneliness is an awesome force. When deprived of contact with one another, we wither up and slowly die from the inside out. You can give a man food and water, sunshine and air; but if you keep him alone, you will destroy him.

Our Lord understood the deep need of our souls for human contact and comfort. We have already seen how the disciples responded like children when the Lord began to prepare them for his departure. "We want to go too!" they begged. You can hear it in Philip's request: "Lord, show us the Father and that will be enough for us" (John 14:8). It's as if Philip were saying, "I just want to make sure there's someone sticking it out here with us." The disciples' dread, just like that of all of us, was rooted in the fear of being alone. And that dread is an ancient one. In fact, I believe being alone is the original "Bad Thing." Do you remember where and when it started? In a garden, long ago.

God had made an amazing universe in six days. Stars glistened in the heavens; planets spun in their orbits. On earth, rivers flowed down mountainsides where wildlife grazed and flowers bloomed. It was paradise, and at the end of each day of creation, God looked over his work and declared it to be "good."

Pause for a moment and consider all that God considers to be good, including the unsightly slug sliming his way across the ground, the creepy tarantula, and the toothy piranha. "Lightning," my son's pet lizard, helped me to realize the breadth of God's definition of *good.*

I found Lightning floating on a leaf in our swimming pool and rescued him from death by chlorine only to be confronted by my seven-year-old son, Riley, who begged to keep him as his pet. Because city life doesn't offer much opportunity to expose our kids to wildlife, I agreed to let Lightning move in. It was one of those little decisions that parents make while saying to themselves, "I mean, it's just a lizard. How much trouble can a lizard be?"

Unfortunately the answer was "plenty." First, our local pet shop assured us that the lizard would die in short order if not supplied with an appropriate indoor habitat. Translated, that means a twenty-dollar plastic terrarium complete with an electrically heated rock so the little fellow's all-important body temperature wouldn't drop too low. But the housing issue was a snap compared to providing meals for our new friend.

The young clerk at the pet shop nearly laughed out loud when I asked for a can of lizard food. "Doesn't come in a can," he snorted. "They eat crickets. Live ones."

He led Riley and me to some glass cages at the back of the shop. Next to a cage of mice and what appeared to be hamsters was a glass container the size of a small aquarium filled with crickets— thousands of them. "You want small, medium, or large?" he asked, getting out a plastic bag and a small net. (As if I knew what size crickets our lizard would eat!)

"Whatever you think," I obliged. "The lizard is only about four or five inches long."

"Medium," he said with an air of zoological assurance. Then he scooped out a dozen insects and told us to feed the lizard a daily diet of two or three crickets.

Riley could hardly wait until we got home to put Lightning into the new reptile condo and feed him. We set it on the kitchen table— a bad move as it turned out. Through a hole in the top of the terrarium, we dropped three unsuspecting "Jimminy Crickets" into the cage. Riley and I watched as they hopped about, exploring their new environment.

We waited for the lizard to do its thing, but nothing happened. It just lay on the "hot rock" nearly motionless.

"Maybe he doesn't see them," Riley said, troubled. But in a moment, one of the little bugs crawled up on the rock directly in front of the lizard. Lightning couldn't possibly have missed it unless he was blind, which conjured up a fresh set of worries in my mind. I had visions of having to spoon-feed an optically challenged lizard. My fears increased as the unsuspecting cricket crawled right onto Lightning's head.

"Dad, look, the lizard is so stupid he doesn't even—" Riley never got a chance to finish that sentence. In a flash so fast that it earned Lightning his name, the lizard whipped up its head, snapped its jaws over the little cricket, and swallowed it whole.

"Wow!" was all Riley could say.

The show got even better. The next cricket to hop to its doom was a bit bigger. The lizard managed only to get the cricket's midsection into its jaws, which left the front legs and hind legs dancing a frightening death jig on either side of Lightning's mouth.

"That is sooo cool!" Riley shrieked.

Cool? There I stood, a parent who had tried hard to protect my child from gratuitous violence on television shows, who had shielded him from the blood and guts of PG-rated movies only to be found watching live-action mortal combat on our breakfast table.

Who provided this spectacle? Who thought it was "good"? You got it! God.

If the bold and bloody cycle of life that God created was "good," how could anything possibly be "bad"? God pronounced one thing in all of creation to be "bad." In fact, what God proclaimed to be "bad" is the same thing the disciples feared in the upper room, the same thing prisoners of war and prisoners everywhere dread. It is being alone. "The LORD God said, 'It is not good for the man to be *alone*'" (Genesis 2:18).

So in response to Adam's loneliness, God gave him a companion, Eve. But though the physical problem of loneliness was thus solved, a spiritual one was created when their sin separated them from God. When they sinned, God cast Adam and Eve out of the garden and into spiritual aloneness.

As painful as physical aloneness is, spiritual aloneness is an even more gruesome specter. Through the prophet Isaiah, God said, "When you spread out your hands in prayer, I will hide my eyes from you; even if you offer many prayers, I will not listen" (Isaiah 1:15). When sin separates us from God, we feel forsaken and are left to wonder if he hears us or cares about us. Unfortunately, the voice that quickly responds to our fears may not be God's, but Satan's. He wants Christians to believe that we have been abandoned, left on the doorstep by Jesus because we don't measure up. Satan wants us to believe that we aren't good enough or smart enough or holy enough to deserve God's favor. He wants us to recoil in shame, feeling that God doesn't want us anymore.

Jesus answered Satan's lie with truth: "I will not leave you as orphans; I will come to you" (John 14:18). Jesus' greatest gift to believers who wait for the Lord's triumphant return is the power of his presence through the Holy Spirit. Jesus promised "another Counselor" who would be with all believers.

Unfortunately, some believers have become leery of this divine guide. They worry about what he might do or how he might cause them to behave. Admittedly, extremes in the charismatic movement have left many people quietly saying, "If that's the Holy Spirit, I'll wait alone for the Lord's return, thank you." But there is no need to worry about this heaven-sent guide if we listen to Jesus' words as he assured his anxious apostles of the reality, role, and results of the Holy Spirit's presence. Those words reveal that we have an amazing partner during our spiritual journey.

The Reality of the Holy Spirit

Counselor.

Comforter.

Guide.

Advocate.

These words and others have been used to describe the full meaning of *paraclete,* the word Jesus chose to describe the special presence of the Holy Spirit in the lives of his followers. The word's simplest meaning is "one who is called alongside another." The image communicated here is derived from the Greek courts in which a defendant might call a friend or counselor to sit beside him during his time of trial and act as his guide and support. That image is an apt picture of the Christian walk. Believers face the accusing world every day, a world that mocks the childish notion of the invisible *Spirit-friend* given to us by our Lord. The world's disbelief should come as no surprise to us because Jesus predicted it when he first gave his disciples the promise of his presence. He clearly said that the world does not hate the Holy Spirit but is simply clueless concerning his presence and his power:

"The world cannot accept him, because it neither
sees him nor knows him." (John 14:17)

And yet we try to explain him to the incredulous world. "He's a force. A power. A feeling deep within." Sound familiar? It can feel like trying to explain radio waves to someone who has never seen or heard a radio. No wonder our non-Christian friends to whom we try to explain the Holy Spirit often respond to us with puzzled smirks and possibly walk away thinking a line from the James Taylor song "Sweet Baby James":

"You can believe it if it helps you to sleep."

But that's when Jesus will whisper to us, "Don't listen to that. They tell you that you are alone, but it's not true. I asked the Father, and he has sent you an amazing companion. You are not alone!"

Desiring to calm the fears and answer the questions of his followers, Jesus gave the disciples in the upper room three key truths about the identity of the Holy Spirit. First, he referred to the Holy Spirit as "another Counselor." The word *another* is an important modifier because it reminded the disciples that they already had a counselor who had come alongside them. His name was Jesus. He had walked with them, taught them, and led them like a good shepherd and a wise friend. Interestingly enough, *friend* is the word Eugene Peterson used in his popular paraphrase of the New Testament, *The Message,* to capture the sense of the Holy Spirit's identity: He is our holy friend. And this new friend was not to bring believers a new or different message; he was sent to affirm the commands of Jesus. "The Holy Spirit…will remind you of everything I have said to you" (John 14:26). In short, the Holy Spirit was to be Jesus with us, yet he is more than that.

Second, Jesus said that the Spirit will be *within* us. A holy being within an unholy human—now there's a wild concept for you. Since Eden, all of humanity has longed for the closeness with God that Adam and Eve threw away. God separated himself from humanity because of his holiness and the repellent nature of sin, but Jesus changed all that. Jesus offered a God-presence that would not be off in the clouds. This presence would not be above us or beside us but within us. The holy friend would live inside each believer.

Best of all, that holy presence would live in believers forever! That's the third truth: Jesus offered no temporary arrangement. The Holy Spirit is not a sometime companion. He is an integral part of every believer.

How we need to remember this truth! Some Christians speak as if the presence of the Holy Spirit comes and goes like a secretive downstairs tenant. "The Spirit was really here tonight," they might say. Or, "The Holy Spirit just showed up. It was awesome." I admit that the Holy Spirit makes his presence more obvious at certain times, but we dare not suggest that he ever leaves the believer of his own accord. That is not consistent with Jesus' words. Christ guarantees that his Spirit will be with us always. He reiterated that promise in the famous line from his final good-bye to the disciples: "And surely I am with you *always*" (Matthew 28:20). Jesus wants us to be assured that once the Holy Spirit moves in, he's not leaving unless we throw him out. Jesus wants us to realize that "I am in my Father, and you are in me, and I am in you" (John 14:20).

By now, the identity of the Holy Spirit should be becoming clear: He is a faithful, "forever friend" who comes from God, is always within us, and will never leave us. Does this sound like Jesus? If you answered yes, you've got the picture, but don't stop there. Christ next described the special function of the Holy Spirit in a Christian's life.

The Role of the Holy Spirit

"I have much more to say to you, more than you can now bear. But when he, the Spirit of truth, comes, he will guide you into all truth" (John 16:12–13).

Those words of Jesus remind me of a bumper sticker I saw the other day: "This Car Is Guided by the Holy Spirit." When I read that on a car in front of me, I didn't know whether to feel more secure or to allow more room between my bumper and his. So much mystery and misinformation exists regarding the guidance function of the Holy Spirit that many Christians find themselves feeling more concerned than comforted.

Our choice of words to describe the work of the Holy Spirit doesn't help: "He got struck by the Holy Spirit." It sounds as if he was hit by a heavenly cement truck! The Book of Acts describes scenes in which the Holy Spirit may indeed have struck someone, but the result was usually death! Praise God, the function of the Holy Spirit in the believer's life is very different. During the Last Supper, Jesus described the Holy Spirit's role as teaching and guiding, simple words to describe an awesome feat.

How does the Holy Spirit guide the believer? Some people have described him as a divine "inner compass" that always points toward God. If the direction of our lives could be set once and forgotten, like setting the time on an alarm clock, the inner guidance of the Holy Spirit would be of little consequence. But there is a constant struggle for power within every believer—a daily battle to do what is right. How does the Holy Spirit help in this fight? There is no better place to turn for help in understanding the Holy Spirit's role in this struggle than to Paul's letter to the Romans.

In Romans 7:22–23, Paul described an internal feud between the Spirit and the flesh. "For in my inner being I delight in God's law; but I see another law at work in the members of my body, waging war against the law of my mind and making me a prisoner of the law of sin at work within my members."

I imagine this struggle in corporate terms. I envision the board of directors of My Life, Inc., as having three members: Mr. B. (my body), Mr. S. (the Holy Spirit), and Mr. M. (my mind). In one chair sits my body, Mr. B. He's the part of me that is oriented toward pleasing the senses, the part that Paul called the "flesh." And he is both completely selfish and very consistent. He always wants what he wants...and he wants it now. Whether it's another handful of candy or another ten minutes of sleep in the morning, Mr. B. always votes for what feels good. Furthermore, he will lie, cheat, and steal to get it. With a straight face, he will offer the most ridiculous arguments, such as, "If you eat the whole pie tonight, I promise we'll skip lunch and dinner tomorrow to make up for it!" Right!

Sitting opposite this manipulative con artist is Mr. S., the Holy Spirit. Like his more selfish opponent, Mr. S. is wonderfully consistent. Unlike Mr. B., however, he is an absolutely straight shooter. He'll level with me and say, "This won't be fun or feel good, but it's the right thing to do." In every setting, he will consistently point me toward what is righteous. His values are those of Christ, and his will comes directly from the Father. "What would Jesus do?" is his favorite question, much to the chagrin of Mr. B.

When a moral dilemma arises, Mr. B. and Mr. S. go at it. Mr. B. passionately argues for passion, and Mr. S. steadfastly advocates Jesus' way. They can argue back and forth for what seems like hours, and when the roll call is taken, each casts votes on the opposite side of almost every issue.

Who casts the tie-breaking vote? Well, occupying the remaining chair is Mr. M., the part of me that wields the gavel and declares a verdict. Unfortunately, my mind is the part of me that is not consistent. My mind can choose to listen to the sweet song of Mr. B. or the clarion call of Mr. S. The inconsistency of my mind is why the Scriptures tell the Christian, "Set your minds on things above" (Colossians 3:2) and "Keep in step with the Spirit" (Galatians 5:25). And that is why we must keep listening for the Spirit's inner voice of integrity.

But our Counselor doesn't stop there. Not only will he guide us concerning the direction we are to go, if we allow him to have full sway in the boardroom of our lives, he will give us the strength to accomplish those God-given calls. The Holy Spirit can do more than advise—he can empower!

The apostles received some powers of the Spirit that I do not expect to receive, such as the ability to write divinely inspired words and to bring miraculous events to pass. Nevertheless, I must not lose sight of the Holy Spirit's ability to empower my life. It is no small promise that through his power I can "put to death the misdeeds of the body" (Romans 8:13). In fact, loving obedience is a sign of the Holy Spirit's power. Jesus said, "Whoever has my commands and obeys them, he is the one who loves me" (John 14:21). Believers who are controlled by the Holy Spirit will follow God's law not only with their minds but with their bodies as well.

Understand that the Holy Spirit will not force us to obey, but like a divine teacher, he will point us to what Jesus has already taught, shining the spotlight on the truth of Jesus' words. Jesus, in turn, points us toward God. When we step back to look at the whole picture, we see that it ends up looking something like this: Christ showed us the nature of God, then he returned to be with the Father. The Holy Spirit came to show us the nature of Jesus, which is the same as the nature of God. Through the presence of the Holy Spirit in our lives, we have the ability to live for God and to live like Jesus. What a comfort it is to know that we are not alone in the battle against our inner desires; our "forever friend" is with us.

And the wonders don't end there. Through our submission to the Holy Spirit, we can demonstrate the truth of God's will to the world. Jesus predicted this when he said that the Holy Spirit would convict and convince the world of sin, judgment, and righteousness (John 16:8). When we allow the wisdom and power of Jesus to have full sway in our lives through the Holy Spirit, we become a convicting sign to the world. We become the proof of Jesus' testimony and the evidence of his gracious authority. As John wrote earlier in his Gospel, "Everyone who does evil hates the light, and will not come into the light for fear that his deeds will be exposed. But whoever lives by the truth comes into the light, so that it may be seen plainly that what he has done has been done through God" (John 3:20–21).

The Results of the Holy Spirit's Presence

We have already noted that holy living is an expected evidence of the Holy Spirit's inhabitance, but Jesus promised an additional blessing. As he finished his introduction of the coming Counselor, he said, "Peace I leave with you; my peace I give you. I do not give to you as the world gives. Do not let your hearts be troubled and do not be afraid" (John 14:27).

The blessing Jesus offered to his disciples—and to us today—is the opposite of fear and loneliness. It is peace. I doubt that the fellows in that upper room saw this one coming. Peace? The more Christ talked about his leaving, the less peaceful they felt. Jesus even pointed out their concern: "Because I have said these things, you are filled with grief" (John 16:6). Like the disciples, we find it difficult to see the benefit of being without the physical presence of Christ. We have those quiet moments of envy when we think about what it must have been like for the disciples to watch him heal and teach people—to actually see, hear, and touch the Lord in the flesh.

But Christ took the opposite tack. He said, in effect, "Don't you see the benefit of my leaving? If I go, you will receive more peace!" But what could possibly be "more peace" than the physical presence of Christ in our midst? It is the spirit presence of Christ in our hearts! Unlike the men who sat *with* the Lord in that upper room, we can sit with him *in* us. His peace, unlike the peace of the world, is truly an inner peace that passes understanding.

Unfortunately, that very peace-bringing presence can become mundane and common place. I am reminded of Thomas a Kempis's comments about the Lord's supper in his fifteenth century Christian classic, *The Imitation of Christ.* He offered that if the communion was only available at one place on the earth and at one time each year, Christians would appreciate it so much more. He wasn't suggesting a plan, mind you. He was underlining a truth. The Lord's supper is taken by millions at different places all over the earth, yet all can commune together simultaneously with their one Lord. Jesus is present with all of them. While he was in the flesh, that would be impossible. But through the Spirit all things are possible.

Do you see what Christ's leaving gave us? As believers, you and I can be at peace with Jesus anytime, anywhere. Because we have the faithful friend always within us, it matters not whether we are locked in a cell or in a frustrating marriage, whether we are trapped in a job that has us feeling lost or in a wheelchair-bound body that leaves us feeling defeated or depressed. Although we are imprisoned for a time in this world, we strain to hear a message tapped out on the walls of the cell next-door. The words are simple, but they are the ones we need until Jesus returns:

He is with us always.... We are not alone!

$\mathcal{S}$ECTION TWO
$\mathcal{W}$ORDS OF $\mathcal{W}$ARNING

A lady driving on a narrow country lane nearly went into a ditch when a car came around the sharp turn ahead of her on the wrong side of the road. When she yelled, "Watch where you're going!" as she passed his window, the offending driver shouted, "Pig!"

The stunned woman shot back, "You're the pig!" and was still fuming in anger when she spun around the curve ahead and nearly crashed into the huge sow that was wallowing in a mud hole in the center of the road.

Some warnings are only understood too late.

Others simply aren't believed. Maybe it is because we have heard words of caution all of our lives:

You play with that BB gun and...

Keep running with those scissors and you're going to...

If you drive that way all the time, you're sure to...

But the cautions offered by Jesus are a bit different. He knew what was coming and what his followers would need to know.

> "Stay close to me."
> "Get along."
> "Do as you're told."

So slow your vehicle down long enough to listen to and consider these few words of caution. They just might save your life.

I am the vine; you are the branches. If a man remains in me and I in him, he will bear much fruit; apart from me you can do nothing. If anyone does not remain in me, he is like a branch that is thrown away and withers; such branches are picked up, thrown into the fire and burned. If you remain in me and my words remain in you, ask whatever you wish, and it will be given you. This is to my Father's glory, that you bear much fruit, showing yourselves to be my disciples.

John 15:5–8

4

STAY CLOSE TO ME

"Do not let go of my hand!"

If anyone around me had been keeping a count, they would have known that was the one-millionth time I had spoken those words to my son in fewer than thirty minutes. But no one was counting or even listening because they didn't speak English—at least not that we could tell. We were in an underground marketplace in Bangkok, Thailand, taking a shortcut to our bus stop. The ceiling was low; the air was heavy. Little booths that served as shops were crammed next to one another in a chaotic jumble. Raw meat was hanging here, and T-shirts of all kinds were hanging there. And over the whole scene, incomprehensible Asian pop music blared from one boom box to another. You would expect Jackie Chan or Bruce Lee to come karate-chopping down the aisle any minute.

And there, in the middle of that, was our little American family. Did we stand out? Not any more than a family of polar bears strolling through downtown Phoenix. I was especially conscious of Riley. At four years of age, his golden-blond curls drew the most stares. I could not forget our taxi driver's warning: "They sell children like him."

At first I thought the driver was just pulling my chain. "Sell them?" I laughed.

"Sure," he said. "The ones who buy children like his hair. His kind sell quickly."

I had not revealed this little chat to my wife for two reasons. First, I didn't put much stock in it. Second, I knew that if she heard a rumor about kiddy-snatchers out there who had a taste for blond boys, we would be on a plane back to the United States before lunch. But when local missionaries confirmed the warning, I made it my job to bodyguard our "Goldilocks."

So I said it once again: "Do not let go of my hand." A tethered four-year-old is not a happy camper, and Riley was growing tired of the restraint. Put a child like him in a weird world full of cool things to look at and neat toys around every turn, and the unstoppable lure of adventure will win out over the immovable parent every time— especially when the parent is distracted.

A booth that sold local carvings caught my eye, and as I haggled with a little, ninety-year-old merchant, my wife grabbed my arm. "Where's Riley?" she demanded. "Right here," I said as I turned around to find out I was wrong. He was gone. The shopkeeper giggled and pointed down one of the aisles. I caught a fleeting glimpse of my son, moving at a full run, headed for some unseen treasure. But he disappeared from view as two fish sellers wheeling cartloads of something from the sea turned into that aisle. I bolted toward the spot where I had seen Riley and sidestepped around the fish carts only to stare down a completely empty aisle. He had disappeared! Within twenty yards, there were easily a dozen places into which he could have ducked, as well as another four aisles down which he could have wandered. All I could do was bellow, "Rileyyyyyy!!!"

Five unbelievably tense minutes later, with the help of a couple of English-speaking merchants, we discovered Riley playing with a shopkeeper's child in the back of a booth of—what else?—Power Ranger figures.

At such a moment, a parent has two competing urges. You want to kiss your child and kick him at the same time. *He's only four years old,* my heart kept telling me; but my mind was saying, *You'd better make him understand.* I settled for thanking God and repeating my mantra one more time: "Riley, listen to Dad. Do not let go of my hand!"

Riley didn't skip a beat. He looked at me and asked, "But *why,* Daddy?"

How do you explain to a child that his life is in danger, that he isn't big enough or smart enough to handle the world on his own? How do you make him understand that without you he would be scared, lost, and crying in no time? If you understand my frustration at that moment, then you relate to what Jesus must have felt as he considered his disciples' future (John 15:1–8).

Jesus was leaving, that much he had explained. The Spirit was coming, that they understood. But as he looked around the table, I wonder if he saw that wandering, childlike look in their eyes. They just weren't getting it. They were scared, but they didn't realize how serious the situation was. If they were to stay safe during his absence, they needed a strong reminder, a clear caution. So Jesus repeated the command, *"Remain in me,"* five times in six verses. These words are Jesus' version of, "Don't let go of my hand!"

How could Jesus make the point in a way they wouldn't forget? Then he spotted it. He picked up the cup that had held the fruit of the vine, or he touched the leaves of a plant's branch that had crept in through the window, and he spoke: "I am the true vine" (John 15:1).

Beginning with the ancient metaphor of the vine that Israel's prophets had used for centuries, Jesus gave his followers a handful of reasons why they must stay close to him. Like a kindergarten teacher who makes all of her students hold hands as they walk through a museum, Jesus wanted to ensure that his followers would stay connected to him. And he knew that in every class, in every generation, there would be the self-assured, little Riley who asks, "Why? Why do I have to hold hands?"

What about you? Do you get tired of holding the Teacher's hand? Sure you do. We all do. We think we're too old for that stuff. We think we're spiritually mature. We think we can handle this Christianity thing. So we wander off to explore and experience new vistas. We go to places we know the Teacher wouldn't let us go. We break things and get dirty. Then we try to fix the situation ourselves. We furtively brush off the dirt and wipe at the stubborn stain. *Nobody needs to know about this little mess,* we hope. But before long, a little mess turns into a big one and we hang our heads. If only we hadn't let go of his hand…

Let's take a moment to sit and listen as the great Teacher explains why it is so important to "remain in him."

Remain in Me Because I Am the True Vine

The story of Israel's relationship with God has more ups and downs than a yo-yo. One minute the Israelites are worshiping him, and the next minute they're putting up Asherah poles or dancing around golden calves. Exodus 32:6 describes their behavior: "They sat down to eat and drink and got up to indulge in revelry." It is as if they could not be faithful to God for any length of time. Theirs was a covenantal relationship with God, a relationship that was to be characterized by faithfulness. Yet the prophet Hosea described Israel in his day as an adulterous woman: "Their mother has been unfaithful and has conceived them in disgrace. She said, 'I will go after my lovers, who give me my food and my water'" (Hosea 2:5).

Hosea's picture is tragic. He married an unfaithful floozy who would hang on to anybody who would buy her a drink. She just couldn't keep her wandering feet at home. Yet God called on Hosea to stand by while she ran around and even sold herself to other men. Thankfully, I know few wives who are anywhere near that godless. But I know even fewer husbands who are anywhere near as godly as Hosea. Even after his wife had prostituted herself into slavery, Hosea went to the market and redeemed her from her harlotry. His action illustrates the way God is willing to redeem us daily. But like Hosea's footloose spouse, we are redeemed at the evening prayer meeting and out sinning again by morning.

What prompts such unfaithfulness? What enables a Christian to slip out the back door of a church and step into the side door of an adult bookstore?

What leads a disciple to let go of the hand of Christ and raise his hand in abuse against his wife or children?

What seduces the believer into dancing with the devil? The words of Christ should give us a clue: "I am the *true* vine" (John 15:1).

Ah! There it is. We become enamored with imitations. The fake vine—the imitation vine—claims to be rooted in something good. It looks succulent and strong, and others who have chosen to drink its nectar look pleasantly filled, so we drink.

What is the name of the false vine?

Money.

Power.

Pleasure.

Fame.

Take your pick. Any of these vines readily offers its sweetness. Just tap into its source and enjoy the taste of passion fruit. Call your own shots. Be your own boss. Have it your way! But the false vines are planted in the condemned dirt of this world. No matter how sweet and filling they may be today, they are destined to dry up and blow away, as will all people who have joined themselves to them.

These false vines may even grow under the guise of religion. In the upper room, Jesus may well have been referring to Jewish leaders and the state religion as the false vine. The Jewish leaders had traded commitment to God for a place in society and a position in the Roman hierarchy. Every disciple of Jesus must be aware that any religion that puts anything in the place of the one true Lord and his Word is not a true vine.

As disciples of Jesus, we must seek out the true Vine, the Vine rooted in the soil of God himself. That Vine's nurturing will last for eternity. The support it gives will carry us through the toughest storms. The love it offers will stand firm through gale-force winds. Accept no imitations. Make sure you're grafted onto the true vine.

Remain in Me Because My Father Is the Gardener

Israel is a land of vineyards. The terrain and climate make them the optimal farming choice for many families. So the disciples immediately understood the importance of the phrase, "My Father is the gardener" (John 15:1). For us, it represents the second sound reason to stay connected to Jesus.

The word translated "gardener" that Jesus used denotes both the owner and manager of a field. He wasn't just a hired hand. The vineyard was his to tend as he saw fit. Then, as in vineyards today, vineyard keepers have but one primary goal: to get the most good fruit possible from the vines under their care. And in a day well before synthetic fertilizers and high-tech growth hormones, the gardener's basic tool was a knife. It was used for both pruning and removing branches. If the distinction between these two purposes escapes you, don't feel bad. I grew up in the city thinking grapes came only in plastic bags. My first trip to the vineyards of central California left me slack-jawed as I saw the rolling hills covered with row upon row of vines. To imagine a vineyard keeper painstakingly reviewing every branch seemed overwhelming to me. Yet that's exactly what Jesus told us his Father does. There are two reasons why the Father uses his knife.

First, fruit-producing branches need pruning. This process involves the strategic removal of some shoots in order to enhance the fruit bearing of the rest of the branch. Pruning is not the wholesale lopping off of branches. It is the art of carefully trimming them back so that the greatest energy goes into the fruit-making endeavor. Christ assured his followers that God had already pruned and cleaned their branches and that he would continue to tend them as they grew.

I can relate to that process. God has used all kinds of circumstances to trim and focus my life. As the Hebrew writer says, "Endure hardship as discipline; God is treating you as sons" (Hebrews 12:7). What kind of hardships can God use to discipline us?

The trial of severe loss.

The pain of unjust treatment.

The frustration of unfulfilled dreams.

All of these, and many others, can be used by the heavenly gardener to prune away that which has kept us from bearing fruit. As one Christian author has written, "Trial only stops when it is useless:

that is why it scarcely ever stops." Yet trials, when not appreciated as part of the pruning process, can be endured for no apparent benefit. As the English writer John Bunyan mused in his memoirs, "There are those that grow ill and well again like beasts, learning nothing from it."

Jesus advised us not to ignore or curse the Father's pruning. Nor should we be surprised by it. Pruning is the gardener's job, and it is our need. There are no "self-pruning" branches. We need his tender cuts in order to keep our lives from becoming like wild, undisciplined brambles.

But pruning is only one use for the gardener's knife. The other is more serious: "He cuts off every branch in me that bears no fruit" (John 15:2). Right next to a branch laden with grapes lies one that is barren. The gardener removes the barren branches lest they inhibit or harm the rest of the plant. Barren branches can block the sun or catch the rain that could have strengthened fruitful branches.

I confess that I don't enjoy these words of Jesus. I long to dwell on the gracious love that he addressed later in John 15. But Jesus knew what we needed. If left to ourselves, we could easily ignore the dark side of the gardener's labors. We would overlook the casting out of dead wood. But if we read much of the New Testament, we can't avoid it. Matthew recorded, "As the weeds are pulled up and burned in the fire, so it will be at the end of the age. The Son of Man will send out his angels, and they will weed out of his kingdom everything that causes sin and all who do evil" (Matthew 13:40–41).

Paul wrote, "This will happen when the Lord Jesus is revealed from heaven in blazing fire with his powerful angels. He will punish

those who do not know God and do not obey the gospel of our Lord
Jesus. They will be punished with everlasting destruction and shut
out from the presence of the Lord and from the majesty of his
power" (2 Thessalonians 1:7–9).

Cutting off barren branches is serious business. The fear of hell
exists for a reason: The gardener will tolerate no barren branches. All
of the great books on the love of God not withstanding, Jesus taught
that barren believers are cut off, cast away, and destroyed. God takes
his labor seriously, and so should we. But before we run and hide
under the covers to escape the gardener's blade, we need to consider
what causes that barrenness.

Remain in Me Because You Can't Bear Fruit Alone

It isn't difficult for a branch to become barren. A careless har-
vester or thoughtless child may unwittingly snap off a branch at its
joint. Although remaining in place, bound to the vine by the
branches surrounding it, the branch is forever severed from the
nutrients it needs to live. It won't wither instantly. In fact, it may
remain green and healthy looking for some time, but it can never
bear fruit. Without drawing nourishment from Jesus, the Vine, it is
destined to shrivel and die.

The importance of remaining fully attached to the vine was a
particularly hard lesson for my youngest son to learn. Spencer is a
kinesthetic child. That's a fancy way of saying that he likes to break
stuff. He learns by touching, holding, and asking inner questions

like, *I wonder how hard I have to pull on this toy's head before it will come off?* Toys can be reassembled, he has learned. But plants are another matter. An afternoon of lovingly nestling twenty-four pansies into the ground in just the right pattern was undone in five minutes by Spencer, who wondered why he couldn't stick those pretty blossoms back on after he pulled them all off!

"You've killed them, Spence," I said. "They won't ever bloom again." He looked as if he truly felt sorry for the dead flowers. I think I even saw a tear form. And I was pleased. Every three-year-old (and some thirty-year-olds) needs to learn that if you break off a living thing from its source of life, it will die.

That's why the image of the fruitless, lifeless, severed branch has such great impact. Jesus didn't end the story with the branch withering and dying. He added an even more terrible end to the parable. When the vineyard keeper finds those kinds of branches, they are "picked up, thrown into the fire and burned" (John 15:6). One minute the fruitless branches are hiding in the plant, and the next minute they are a puff of smoke and a pile of cinders. Jesus foreshadows the ultimate judgment scene in the vineyard bonfire. The moral is stark and stern: get disconnected from the vine and get torched.

Images such as these can leave young Christians quivering in their wet, baptismal garments, but there is no need for abject fears when we consider why those branches were burned. The gardener burned them because they lost their connection to Christ. They weren't a little lazy or struggling to overcome a particular sin. They hadn't just arrived late to church or forgotten their memory verses.

They had become disconnected. They were cut off and unattached. They had ceased to pledge their allegiance to Christ and depend on him for life. They weren't part of him anymore. They had forgotten that without Christ no one can do anything.

In a do-it-yourself world, it's easy to lose sight of the truth that we can do nothing apart from Christ. Look at our society. We believe there is no problem we can't solve, no challenge we can't meet. Consider our track record:

> *Social injustice?*
> —We'll pass civil rights laws.
> *Gang problems among the young?*
> —We'll open private schools and build juvenile
> correction facilities.
> *Unrest across the globe?*
> —We'll send in Stinger missiles and
> topnotch troops.

We each stride through life like a modern-day Alexander the Great, boasting, "I came. I saw. I paid to have it fixed!"

But what have we fixed? One look around the globe should tell us that Jesus was right. Without his divine wisdom and merciful grace, we are lost and fruitless. Like branches that have been snapped off the vine, we can't bear lasting fruit no matter how hard we try.

That is exactly what Jesus wanted every believer to know: We must remain in him, or we will die. But more than that, if we do remain in him, we will live...and live fruitfully.

$\mathscr{R}$emain in Me Because If You Do I'll Make You Fruitful!

I used to believe that being a do-gooder was the supreme goal of a Christian disciple, so each day I set out to do good. Mine was a basic boy-scout Christianity:

> Be helpful.
> Be kind.
> Be courteous.

The problem was, I found this regimen very difficult to maintain. First, my efforts were often viewed as weakness, and I was taken advantage of. My kindness was abused; my helpfulness was overused. And to make matters worse, I was often unappreciated. Sometimes my good deeds went totally unnoticed, and I was reduced to pointing them out in hopes of receiving proper recognition.

The path out of this works-based futility came through a change of focus. I had been focusing on the wrong thing. So instead of dwelling on the good deeds I needed to do, I began to focus on the good Lord whom I had pledged to follow. When I focused on remaining in him, on knowing and trusting his Word, my do-gooding came more naturally and less painfully.

All I needed to do was make sure I stayed connected to Christ. If I did, the good stuff would flow. Jesus said, "If a man remains in me and I in him, he will bear much fruit; apart from me *you can do nothing*" (John 15:5). Pretty blunt language, don't you think? Jesus didn't say that I could only do a little or a bit less apart from him.

Nope. Jesus made sure I came face to face with the truth: Without him, I am an absolute do-nothing!

Trying to bear fruit on our own is like trying to turn on a light that isn't plugged in. Our first response is to replace the bulb. If the light still doesn't work, we might try wiggling the switch or fiddling with the socket. But sooner or later, we'll check the plug. If it isn't plugged in, no replacement bulb or new connection will fix the problem.

So it is with Christ. Without him, we lack the power to produce the light this world needs. Without him, we are like lightless lamps, lumps of saltless salt, and fruitless branches.

But with him…Ahhhh, there's the joy!

With him, I will be fruitful—He promises it.

With him, I will be effective—He guarantees it!

The trick is to remain in him and never forget the importance of that connection. When you feel a power drain, don't just run out to do something. First check your connection to the Vine. When life feels barren and limp, don't just bear down and try harder. Reaffirm your connection to the root and renew your attachment to the source. Some days I think that every Christian church needs a sign up front that reads, "It's Jesus, stupid!" We may not need more training to be more effective. We may just need more of the Savior.

Finally, let's not forget where the credit should go when good things do happen: "This is to my Father's glory, that you bear much fruit" (John 15:8). When our branches are heavy with the good fruit of merciful deeds and saved people, remember who brought it all to pass. Paul reminded us that we may plant and water, but God makes things grow (1 Corinthians 3:6–7). All the kudos and honors go to him. If we give God the glory and remain in the love and guidance of his Son, we are promised effective prayers, fruitful branches, and joyous lives.

All that for not letting go of his hand.

Thirty-eight years ago, there was another lost boy and another worried father. I was about Riley's age, walking through a huge store with my father when an aisle of toys caught my eye. Letting go of my dad's hand for just a minute, I slipped over to examine an especially cool truck, the kind that could both pick things up and dump them out. I couldn't have been there more than a minute when I turned around to show it to my dad.

He was gone, nowhere to be seen.

I panicked.

This was the moment I had worried about. My dad had seen his opportunity and seized it. He had ditched me! So I did the only thing I knew to do. I started yelling his name.

"Daaadyy!" Fifty men whose first name happened to be "Daddy" peeked around the end of the aisle, but none of them was mine.

My panic increased. I began wondering what they did with leftover kids at K-Mart. Did they sell them the next day as a blue-light special? "Attention K-Mart shoppers. On aisle twelve…"

"Daaadyy!" It was louder and longer this time, and this time it worked. I recognized a balding head as he peered around the end of a rack of plastic action figures. I darted for him like a heat-seeking missile and hit him in the midsection doing about forty miles per hour. He didn't even budge. He just hoisted me up in his arms and held me tightly. "Daddy," I cried into his cheek, "don't ever leave me like that!"

He smiled and said, "How about we make a deal, son? You don't leave me, and I won't leave you."

I accepted the deal. I suggest you do the same.

As the Father has loved me, so have I loved you. Now remain in my love. My command is this: Love each other as I have loved you.

John 15:9, 12

5

GET ALONG

Okay, history buffs, here's one for you: Which all-consuming issue nearly divided the Russian Orthodox Church in October 1917? Sounds easy, right? That was the time of the Bolshevik Revolution, the historic uprising of the underclass that toppled the czars and planted the seeds of Communism. Surely the Russian Orthodox Church was debating capitalism or the divine right of kings. They must have been wrestling with the needs of the poor and how the church could respond to them without overlooking its responsibility to respect the appointed rulers. It had to be something like that, right?

Wrong.

In about 1917, the state church of mother Russia was engaged in a divisive argument over...robes. Yes, you read it right: robes.

There was a difference of opinion regarding the type of robes the priests would wear. It had to do with the color of the cloth and the design of the stole. The church folk had a doozie of a fight over their clerics' clothes while the rest of the country was shedding blood over freedom and food. Is it any wonder the church was ineffective in maintaining a powerful Christian witness in the face of Communism a few decades later?

If the church of Jesus Christ has been given to any one sin through the years, it would have to be the sin of discord and its related vices. Some church people can fight at the drop of a collection plate. Churches have split over the way the children are taught during Sunday school or the number of cups in the communion tray. Brothers and sisters in the faith have been reduced to cussing each other out over the style of worship or the design of the cross that would (or would not) adorn the sanctuary. Just name an issue, and you can find a congregation that has divided over it.

Do you ever wonder why this is true? I suppose the simple answer is the best: It's natural. What child has ever had to be taught to be greedy or demand his or her own way? Consider how long it has been since you heard an anxious mother say to a friend, "I'm just so worried about little Rodney. He's too nice to the other children at preschool. I'm constantly having to tell him, 'Tease her, son. Pull her hair or pinch her!'" Since birth, we have a self-serving mechanism that works like a charm.

Consider newborns. People speak of babies as being delightful little doses of heaven. I beg to differ. Watch a baby. A baby is the picture of selfishness. It wants food when it's hungry, and if you dare to make it wait, it will make your life miserable. When a baby wants to be held, you'd better drop anything else in your hands—no matter how important—or it will give you what for in a high-pitched wail you won't want to hear again.

As a baby grows into a toddler, things don't get much better. They just get more verbal. The first words out of most toddlers' mouths aren't "Mommy" or "Daddy" but "Gimme!"

I remember watching an unfortunate parent fight with a selfish child in a shopping mall. The tyke had spotted something he wanted in a toy store and was demanding it with all his lung power. His frustrated mom was trying to quiet the tyke, saying, "Willie, please don't yell. We don't have time to go back there now. We'll come back later."

This wasn't cutting it with Willie. He went into full tantrum mode—feet flying, arms flailing, and head shaking. It was quite a show, and I had a front-row seat. I wasn't the only shopper who had stopped my window gazing to do a little Willie watching. Some mothers looked on in pity, while others shook their heads in open condemnation of this eight-year-old spectacle. Undeterred, Willie finished his fit by flopping down cross-legged in the middle of the mall walkway and shouting, "If you don't take me back there right now, I'm gonna hold my breath till I die."

Fifty people in the mall nearly hollered back, "Do it, Willie! Put all of us out of our misery!" When you see that kind of raw self-centeredness, you don't have to wonder long why Christians have a hard time cooperating: We're human. You also don't have to wonder why Jesus thought it was important to give his followers a stern lecture about getting along before he left them.

"My command is this," he said. "Love each other as I have loved you" (John 15:12). No more challenging task could be encompassed in eight words. As a parent, I often condense his message to just two words: Get along! When you leave very young children with a babysitter, they need the reassuring words, "I'll be back. Don't be afraid." But when your children get older, there's a different concern on your heart. You leave them with the words, "Just don't fight!" Like a wise parent, Jesus knew that the time would come when the fears he had allayed by his earlier comments would be forgotten and the hope he promised by his coming again would be overlooked. Then the children of God would need the command of their Lord that supersedes all others: "Love each other...whether you like it or not!"

Scant minutes after giving this command, Jesus was prostrate in the garden, alone with death, weeping and praying for himself and his disciples. In the middle of that prayer, he offered a few words for all believers, even you and me. "My prayer," he prayed, "is not for them alone. I pray also for those who will believe in me through their message, that all of them may be one, Father, just as you are in me and I am in you. May they also be in us so that the world may believe that you have sent me" (John 17:20–21).

One powerful purpose behind Jesus' command to lovingly get along and forge unity from compassion was to show the world that Jesus was God's Son. If we can't learn to get along with one another, how is the world supposed to believe that we have been touched by the Messiah? When the unbelieving masses look at the splintered and divided church, they laugh out loud. And why shouldn't they? If this is the best peace that the Prince of Peace can produce, he may as well turn in his crown.

When we fight and bicker, we become living proof that Jesus doesn't have the power to change lives. Oh, he may be able to get folks to act nicely for an hour on Sunday, but just watch them the rest of the week! Our lack of love for one another cuts the legs out from under our evangelism and makes a mockery of our testimony.

So how do we become people of love? How can we be transformed into an authentic community of caring people who speak to the world about real love? I believe the answer lies in the words of Christ. So let's wade into the deep waters of Christ's command and immerse ourselves in the depths of its truth.

*J*esus' Love Comes from Another World

Jesus didn't use the word *love* lightly. He modified it in an extraordinary way. He told us that we are to love one another as he has loved us. That would be challenging enough, but Jesus also revealed the source of that love. Through a chain of simple statements, he traced back the lineage of the love he commands and unveiled its holy family history. The love of which Jesus spoke began a long way from here. You won't find its source in romance novels or erotic movies. No, this love began in another world, in a perfect kingdom ruled by a perfect King. Jesus described this love when he said, "As the Father has loved me, so have I loved you" (John 15:9).

God love.

Divine love.

Supernatural love.

This love came from the heart of the Creator and flowed freely to his only Son. The mystery of the godhead keeps us from fully seeing or appreciating this love, but we can at least get close. We can understand the parent-child devotion to which Christ compared this love: "as the Father has loved me."

Before I became a parent, I wondered what the big deal was about kids. As some of my friends married and started having babies, I marveled at the metamorphosis they went through. They went gaga over the goo-goo stuff. "The Kid" became the center of their lives.

Suddenly there were no more late-night movie runs because "the kid needs to be in bed by 8:00 P.M." There were no more weekend ski trips because "we couldn't think of leaving the kid with someone else overnight!" Life, in its previous style, was over. The new parents' full-time focus was on "The Kid."

To my way of thinking, their perception of "The Kid" was downright psychotic. I'll never forget the first of my friends who had pictures of his newborn from the delivery room.

"Want to see a picture of my new baby?" he asked.

My experience with other proud parents told me he wasn't really asking. I was gonna see this snapshot whether I liked it or not. So I played along and said, "Sure, I'd love to."

He whipped it out of his wallet and stuck it right under my nose.

I nearly fainted

I was expecting one of those cutesy baby pictures they do at the shopping malls. You know what I mean—the photos where the kid is dressed in his fluffiest outfit and they stick stuffed animals around him to hold him up. Those pictures manage to make every baby look like it just crawled off a Gerber jar. But not this picture. This piece of work had been taken literally at the moment of birth.

You couldn't see Mom, but the baby was still attached by the umbilical cord. The child hadn't even been washed. It was covered with a bloody mucus. I would learn years later that this is typical of all newborns and that the nurses just wash the stuff off before you take the baby out to show Grandma in the waiting room. But no prephoto bath for my buddy's baby. He snapped his kid's Polaroid bloody mucus and all. To make matters worse, my friend's child had a tough time getting through the birth canal. That process had squeezed the baby's head into a point sharp enough for a #2 pencil. The end result was a photograph that looked like a guy holding a bloody lizard with a red rope coming out of its stomach.

I didn't know what to say. I finally stammered, "I-I-I'm so sorry. W-W-What's wrong with it?"

"Wrong with it?" he laughed. "She's beautiful!" To prove it, he kissed the photo with a loud smack. I thought I would throw up.

Since that time, my wife and I have had three bloody lizards of our own, so I now completely understand my friend's feelings. We, too, are head over heels in love with our kids. No matter how dirty, ornery, or messy they are, no matter which window they have broken or which neighbor kid they've punched, they are our kids and we love them.

That, in a small way, illustrates the kind of love the heavenly Father has for his Son. That's why even when Jesus went to the grave covered with the bloody mucus of the sins of humanity, the God who could not abide sin raised him from the dead anyway. He would not let his "Holy One see decay" (Psalm 16:10). God would not abandon his boy.

It is that out-of-this-world, over-the-top kind of love to which Jesus calls us. As a Christian, I am to have for you no less love than the Father has for the Son.

I am to *see* you through the compassion-colored lens by which a parent views his or her child.

I am to *forgive* you with the ease and grace by which a mother forgives the daughter she loves.

I am to *tolerate* you with the patience and fortitude by which a father greets the endless missteps and mistakes of his slowly maturing offspring.

I am to *care for* you with the endless gentleness that a loving parent demonstrates to a sick or hurting child.

Jesus' words stand as our constant example: "As the Father has loved me, so have I loved you" (John 15:9).

*J*esus Loves with a Savior's Love

But Jesus raised the bar another notch with yet another set of unassuming words: "Love each other as I have loved you" (John 15:12). The compassionate love of a parent is perhaps surpassed only by the unconditional love of our Savior. It was in that same room that Jesus had taken a bowl and towel and by washing his disciples' feet had "showed them the full extent of his love" (John 13:1). When no servant appeared to handle the customary and menial task of washing their feet, Jesus had taken the servant's role upon himself. He had knelt and scrubbed every toe—even the ten belonging to Judas.

Now there's an image for you. I don't know why some great painter or sculptor hasn't tackled that one: Jesus washing the feet of Judas. Maybe it's just too unimaginable, even for an artist. What expression would you put on Judas's face? A self-assured grin? A smug frown of disgust? Was he really so cold-hearted and possessed by Satan that he could sit there and watch the Lord of all the earth wash his feet while he pondered how to use the betrayal money? And how would an artist portray Jesus? Would his head be bowed in quiet commitment? Would his eyes be closed so as to betray nothing about the betrayer with his gaze? I don't think so.

I think Jesus was looking right at Judas.

I think Jesus was staring into his eyes.

And I think Jesus was crying.

Jesus knew the hell Judas was heading for, the torment he was buying for himself. Yet Jesus cared anyway. Jesus would die on the cross for all such men because that's the kind of love he had—a Savior's love.

The Savior's love is unlike ours, for it is not driven by *ifs* or *whens* such as "I'll love you *if* you treat me right" or "I'll love you *when* you straighten up." The Savior's love is not conditioned by right behavior or a good performance. It pays no attention to IQ, bank balance, or skin color. It is blind to appearance and deaf to tone. It cares not about heritage, reputation, or rap sheet.

On the contrary, the Savior's love says, in effect, "I'll die for you while you still wallow in your sins. I'll give my life for you while you give your time to the delights of the flesh. I'll go to the cross for you knowing that you wouldn't go across the street for me. I'll do all of that because I love you so."

What a love he has for us! But he doesn't want the story to end there.

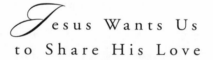

Jesus Wants Us to Share His Love

The love that started in the halls of heaven and progressed through the body of our Savior on a cross finishes its course with us. Yes, us! We are the last link in this divine chain—and surely the weakest. If we fail to pass this baton to other people, all is lost. And the only way we can pass on this holy heritage is by loving one another.

I am not alone in suggesting that everything comes down to loving one another. Paul warned the Corinthians that without love all the sermons and church talk were nothing but "a resounding gong or a clanging cymbal" (1 Corinthians 13:1). Without love, all the giving and doing profits us nothing. Even faith cannot work its wondrous potential without love.

Because of this, I'm convinced that we must commit to love as to nothing else. We must place it in the supreme position of our hearts and minds. We must marshal all our strength to fulfill this one task: loving one another.

But let me pause here and explore an often-overlooked requirement that enables us to love. Allow me, if you will, to ask you a personal question: When was the last time you let the Lord *love you?*

We spend much time in prayer explaining our faults and begging for God's mercy and aid, but we often overlook the great power that comes when we simply let him love us. He wants to love us. He died to love us. And if we are to love other people as he calls us to, we must first relax in his loving embrace.

When we have known his tender forgiveness and rested in his unconditional acceptance, then—and only then—are we truly ready to face a frustrating spouse or a cantankerous brother with renewed vigor and fresh compassion. Unless we have accepted and experienced God's divine, selfless love, we will be unable to offer it to others. We cannot give away that which we have never received.

There's one more thing. We must decide to love right now. I'm not suggesting that you lay down this book and rush out to hug someone this moment. I mean that this kind of love is a predecided love. It is an "already love." This kind of love isn't something you choose in the heat of emotions or in the haze of weariness. Those are the times when less noble options come to mind. No, this kind of love requires you to make a decision before your eyes meet the person you must love. This kind of love is a commitment you forge before your feet hit the floor each morning. It is saying to everyone we meet, "I've already decided to love you."

A fellow minister tells about a counseling situation he will never forget. The young lady who made the appointment, Janice, was the daughter of one of his best friends, Carl. When she demanded his secrecy about even coming to see him, his fears began to mount. And when she walked into his office with Tommy, the young man she had been dating for some time who looked like he was heading to the gas chamber, he knew his fears weren't unfounded.

Their story spilled out in a gush of tears and remorse. She was pregnant, and Tommy was the father. They had told no one else about their situation. They had decided that eloping was their only choice.

Janice pushed a note across my friend's desk. "I want you to give this to Dad," she said. "Tell him I'm sorry."

"I won't do it," my wise friend responded. "You'll have to take this to him yourself."

"I can't. He'll kill me. He'll kill Tommy. You don't understand."

"It may be you two who don't understand. You see, I'm a parent too." And with that, he began to quietly convince her to face her father and trust his love for her. It took thirty minutes before

Tommy's courage melted. He was having no part of this scene and left in a huff. My friend ended up driving Janice to her father's business himself.

Upon entering the father's plush suite of offices, my minister friend told the secretary to hold all of Carl's calls. Then they walked into his private office unannounced. Carl was in the middle of a business call, but one look at my friend's face and his daughter's red eyes brought it to an abrupt end. "I'll call you back. I've got something here I need to deal with." He pushed a button on the phone, turned his gaze on my friend, and asked, "What's up, Stan? What's going on?"

"Just sit down, Carl. Janice has something she needs to tell you."

But Janice couldn't tell her father. Each time she opened her mouth, it was only to cry a little more. Her father must have seen the dread in her eyes. He slowly said the words, "Are you pregnant?" The fresh gush of tears from his daughter confirmed it.

Before my friend could move to intervene, Carl grabbed Janice by the shoulders and held her with a vice-like grip. "Look at me!" he demanded. "Look at me!"

When her tear-filled eyes met his, he took a deep breath and spoke these words my friend has committed to memory: "I am so angry...and hurt...and disappointed. And...I am still your father, and we will get through this together." Then it was Carl who could not speak for weeping. His daughter collapsed into her father's embrace, and they both sunk down onto a couch, holding each other and saying, "I'm sorry" and "I love you."

At that instant, something snapped inside my friend. *I'm a parent too,* he thought. His own daughter, born less than two months after Janice, was home for a long weekend. He excused himself with a promise to meet both of them the next evening and dashed to his car. He drove straight home and bounded upstairs to his daughter's bedroom. She was sitting on her bed, folding some clothes she had washed.

"Hey, Dad, what are you doing here?"

"I've got to ask you an important question, honey," my friend began. "What would you do if you got pregnant?"

She looked at him aghast. "Dad! Frank and I aren't even dating anymore. And besides, I'm being good!"

"No, no, baby. That's not it at all. I know you're a good girl. I just want to know, what would you do if you were pregnant?"

She was still confused. "I can't believe you are asking me this. Don't you trust me?"

"Of course I trust you. Just go with me on this, okay? It's one of your old man's crazy notions. Just answer the question. If you were pregnant…what would you do?"

She paused, and my friend prayed a silent prayer.

"Well, I suppose the first thing I would do would be to pray."

"That's good," he choked out, "but what would you do next?"

"I guess then I would…" There was an agonizing pause. "…come tell you and Mom."

My friend let out a huge sigh and sank to his knees. Taking his daughter's hand, he locked his eyes on hers and said, "And let me tell you what I've already decided I would do. I would cry and probably be very hurt and angry. But I am your father, and I would stand by you all the way."

Does anyone in your world believe that of you? Has anyone heard that kind of love commitment from your lips? If we are to make it together from here to heaven, we must share that kind of love with each other. Christ will accept nothing less.

If you obey my commands, you will remain in my love, just as I have obeyed my Father's commands and remain in his love. I have told you this so that my joy may be in you and that your joy may be complete.

John 15:10–11

6

DO AS YOU'RE TOLD

The young lady squirmed silently in her chair and nervously twirled a lock of her hair. "Is there something wrong with the vows?" I asked.

Up until that point, the premarital counseling sessions had gone as expected. This was the last session before the wedding, which would take place in three weeks. I had outlined the ceremony for the couple and had just finished reviewing the vows I like to use. This part used to be a no-brainer. Everybody used basically the same wedding vows, a set of words crafted in England sometime during the eighteenth century: "Do you, John Smith, take this woman, Toni Brown, to be your lawfully wedded wife…" and so on.

But since the free-spirited sixties, many couples have written their own vows. Through the years, I've had to read some weird ones with a straight face, such as:

John, you are Toni's eucalyptus tree.
Do you promise to grow by her in shade and storm,
To never let your leaves fall on her trunk
or let your fallen branches choke her roots?

I'm convinced that vows such as these may sound hip at the moment, but they end up as embarrassments on wedding videos years later. The day will come when a child will look incredulously at his parents and say, "Dad, you promised to be a tree?"

The couple sitting before me had wisely opted to use the more traditional vows, but something was clearly bugging the bride-to-be. She finally spoke. "I don't want that word in there," she declared, pointing to the offending word on the copy I had given her. "The rest is fine, but I don't want to say that." I didn't have to look to know which word it was: *obey.* She wasn't the first bride who wanted to strike that line from her vows. Although "I promise to love, honor, and obey" has been spoken by countless women in white, many modern women find the phrase both outdated and out of the question!

No wonder. In our culture, *obey* has become a four-letter word. It has been linked to images of forced marches and indentured servants. In many people's minds, *obey* is the tool of the dictator and the taskmaster. To obey is perceived as the opposite of being free, and freedom is the currency of the realm.

So we've replaced "do as you are told" with "please, consider choosing to comply." We've done away with the rules and replaced them with suggestions. For example, Johnny doesn't spell words incorrectly anymore, he just offers *creative alternatives.* Homosexuality isn't sin—it's an *alternative lifestyle.*

All the while, the "let-me-be-me" crowd urges us onward with idyllic images of a utopian society in which everyone is free to do as they see fit. No rules to hold us back! No authorities to obey! Nothing but universal freedom! And how we love the promise of freedom.

Free love!

Free sex!

Free Willy!

If it has *free* in front of it, we'll buy it. More than that, we'll claim it as an inalienable right. We will fight for the right not to have to fight and not to *have to* do anything. Without the "have tos" in our world, we believe, we will be free to evolve into the peace-loving, free creatures we are intended to be.

This kind of thinking has led our culture to throw out traditions and morals as if they were plague-infested bedding. Out with the old and in with…nothing! We want no new morals, no new codes. We believe that any law, any restriction, is tyranny. The assumption is, you do what feels good—and I will too. It'll be wonderful!

At the same time, we wonder why a generation of kids vacillates between anarchy and neo-Nazism. Why would they accept the dark visions of the Gothic culture, dressed in black from head to toe and wearing an attitude to match? Why would thousands of them enslave themselves to cults that put extremely strict demands on their followers? What happened to the utopia that was promised if we just struck the word *obey* from our vocabulary?

Which brings me back to my blushing bride-to-be.

"You can leave out any word you want," I said quietly, "but before you do, may I show you something Jesus said?" I opened a Bible to John 15:10–11:

> If you obey my commands, you will remain in my love, just as I have obeyed my Father's commands and remain in his love. I have told you this so that my joy may be in you and that your joy may be complete.

"Why do you think Jesus spoke the words *love, obey,* and *joy* in the same breath?" I asked her.

The question I posed is one all of us ought to ponder. What is the connection between love, obedience, and joy? In this all-important final discourse with his apostles, there must be a reason why Jesus joined the concepts of obedience and joy in a truly holy matrimony. What God has joined together, let not man put asunder.

In stunning simplicity, Christ let his disciples see that the joy they longed for in life was forever connected to obedience and that obedience was part of love. Our world desperately needs this message, but before we carry it to the world, we'd better take it to the church. The same "anti-obedience" virus that has plagued our culture has infected the church as well. Certainly God does not approve of abusive, authoritarian religious practices. I will make no argument for a toxic faith that substitutes pleasing a church hierarchy for pleasing Jesus. However, Jesus clearly warned that when we throw out obedience, we throw joy out with it. Listen carefully as he makes the case for the joy of obedience.

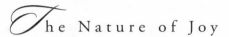

The Nature of Joy

There's a portrait of Jesus I love. I don't know who the painter is, but his vision of the Lord is both shocking and sublime: He captures Jesus laughing. The artist portrays Jesus with his head thrown back in the full joy of a hearty guffaw. The first time I saw the painting, I didn't know whether to buy it or run for cover before the lightning hit. *Jesus laughing?* I thought. *Doesn't this guy know what a serious ministry Jesus had? Doesn't he realize that each step Christ took brought him one step closer to the cross? A laughing Jesus indeed!* But as I have studied Christ's words and looked at his life, I have come to believe that the artist may have been on to something when he or she chose to represent a happy Lord. Consider some of the evidence:

I bring you good news of great *joy* that will be for all the people. (Luke 2:10)

I say these things…so that they may have the full measure of my *joy* within them. (John 17:13)

I have come that they may have *life,* and have it to the *full.* (John 10:10)

You have been faithful with a few things…. Come and share your master's *happiness!* (Matthew 25:21)

Rejoice in that day and leap for *joy*, because great is your reward in heaven. (Luke 6:23)

You will grieve, but your grief will turn to *joy*. (John 16:20)

Even before his birth, Christ brought joy to the earth. We can trace the ministry of Jesus across Israel by following a trail of joy. We see a blind man who can now see shouting with joy. We see a lame man who can now walk leaping for joy. We see a widow whose son is back from the dead weeping with tears of joy.

Consider also Jesus' very first miracle. He turned water into wine. Now I ask you, is whipping up more Chablis for a wedding bash what you would have chosen for Jesus' premiere miracle? Not me. I was taught in Bible class that this was to show Christ's authority over inanimate objects. (I'm not sure who cooked that one up.) And try explaining this miracle to the same middle-schoolers to whom the week before you taught the lesson on the evils of alcohol. I'll confess, had I been on the angelic Miracle Planning Committee, I would have voted down this miracle in a harp beat. Water to wine? No way. Nonalcoholic or not, wine sends the wrong message.

But God thought differently. He chose to let Jesus begin his miracle ministry by creating more joy. It was to be a hallmark of his life. Like the bread crumbs Hansel and Gretel dropped, Jesus left happy folks in his wake from Galilee to Jerusalem. If you wanted to find him, all you had to do was follow the line of grinning people!

Of course, Christ's critics complained about his tendency to create joy. "Why don't your disciples fast?" they asked. Apparently, his disciples seemed far too happy! So Jesus answered, in effect, "I'm with them. They can't help it." Indeed, Jesus had that effect on people. Why else did the children run to him with such delight that his disciples felt the need to shoo them away? Children don't flock to the grouchy and dour. They run to the joyful. They gravitate to the grinning.

And the joy didn't stop there. It continued to exhibit itself in the lives of the apostles. When the Holy Spirit filled the disciples on Pentecost, he brought not only power, but joy! Paul declared, "The fruit of the Spirit is love, joy, peace...." (Galatians 5:22). For joy came not only through the miracles they performed but through the transforming message they preached.

The first Christians were harbingers of joy, and the early church was a rejoicing church. Despite the persecutions that quickly arose, the early Christians fully believed that the story of Jesus Christ was the ultimate good news. "And they went on their way rejoicing" became the standard tag line for the early believers. They preached the joy of the Lord and offered his eternal blessing to anyone who would choose him. Happiness was so symptomatic of the first Christians that first-century writer Hermas refers to the Holy Spirit as the "Happy Spirit."

So how did many of us become so dour? Have we willfully misrepresented Christ? Perhaps it happened because of all the crucifixion art we display in our churches and homes. Jesus was only on the cross for a few hours, but I would wager that crucifixion images outnumber all other images of Jesus by three to one. And when we portray him before he went to the cross, it is with a clouded look of woe or kneeling in the garden in great sorrow.

Perhaps we Christians become dour because of the way in which we often worship. "Sit still and be solemn" are the unspoken rules of many worship services. This solemnity and austerity will suck the wind out of any happy new believer's sails. As Arthur Gossip wrote in his treatise on John's Gospel, "But would anyone, stumbling in, sense that here are people who have made a glorious discovery and are thrilled and joy possessed?" He asks a good question.

But our demeanor is our choice, not Jesus' plan. He desires for us to have his joy, to experience the full measure of his happiness. But while we're seeking this soul-deep happiness, we must remember that Satan offers an appealing plan for joy as well. It's called sin.

The Needs of Sin

One of the biblical words we translate "sin" is *hamartia*. It is an archery term that means "missing the mark." The image *hamartia* conveys is that of an archer who aims at the target but whose arrow is blown off course by the wind. Do you see the truth hidden here? Sin is an off-target attempt at reaching happiness. It is crossing over the lines that God has drawn. At its root, sin is a failed attempt to find joy. How many times have we seen sin miss the mark?

I thought this affair would make me happy.

I was just looking for some happiness, and the drugs seemed to provide it.

I didn't want to leave my husband, but I just had to find some joy in my life.

I really believed that if I had enough money I would be fulfilled—truly happy.

Disobeying God *needs* to masquerade as freedom and joy. But as in *The Phantom of the Opera,* horrors unspeakable lie behind that ceramic smile. If you have any doubt about the horror behind sin's joy, just ask the burned-out junkie lying on the street corner or the depressed executive tossing back his fifth martini. They did not, as Jesus said, taste of "my joy." They drank from a phony holy grail and swallowed a bitter potion indeed.

But how are such bright, willing souls duped? Evil lures them into its grasp by the deceit of disobedience. I love the way C. S. Lewis described evil: "a gray day in a British midland city." The first time I heard his description, I didn't understand it. I expected a description of evil that was closer to the frightening demons of a Frank Peretti novel or a Stephen King movie. I envisioned evil as the Boogieman, Dracula, and Freddie Krueger all rolled into one.

Then I began to understand. What I envisioned is just what evil *wants* us to think. Evil seeks to paint disobedience and sin as a powerful, passionate, romantic ideal. It wants us to lust after evil as the desirable taboo, the delicious deceit. Evil needs that daring image to lure us to join it. Evil cannot appear as it is: a boring slavery to one sin after another.

The writer of Proverbs knew the nature of evil well. That is why he warned that wickedness and folly would come as an alluring woman, enticing the naive to ignore wisdom's rules. She is "the wayward wife with her seductive words, who has left the partner of her youth and ignored the covenant she made before God" (Proverbs 2:16–17). And evil doesn't want you to see her without her makeup on.

Evil needs several things in order to make disobedience look good. It needs the darkness in which to hide the awful results of sin that will show up at dawn. It needs the neon lights and loud dress to distract its victims from the drudgery that awaits anyone who partners with it. It needs the raucous music of discord and the noise of passion to keep its latest recruits from hearing the wails of previous victims.

And what awaits the one who succumbs to evil's come-on? Sin will tell you that it wants only a room in the back—just a little corner where it can hang its hat. "You keep going to church and go right on saying your prayers," Evil whispers. It then promises, "I'll just hang back here in the shadows, waiting for a quiet moment when you can come and play." Don't you believe it!

Sin doesn't want a room. It wants to reign!

Sin is not a way to live. It is a way to die!

Sin is not the path to freedom. It is the path to slavery!

And sin will not rest until it has covered every inch of your life with its drab fog of guilt. Sin will slowly suck the joy, the vibrancy, and the very life from you until the whole world looks black and gray and nothing seems worth living for. Paul's warning rings so true: "Therefore do not let sin reign in your mortal body so that you obey its evil desires. Do not offer the parts of your body to sin, as instruments of wickedness.... Don't you know that when you offer yourselves to someone to obey him as slaves, you are slaves to the one whom you obey?" (Romans 6:12–13, 16).

Slavery is the end of the road of disobedience. What began as rebellion against the rules ends up being servitude without hope or joy. The prodigal son in the pigpen didn't feel that his life was full of glamour. As he considered having a McSlop sandwich for lunch, it dawned on him: *This isn't what I signed up for! What happened to the glitz, the girls...the joy?*

The good news is, joy is still available. All the joy we could ever want awaits us, but it is down a route we least expect. During the Last Supper, Jesus put up a surprising road sign. He revealed that the path to joy is found in obedience.

The Power of Obedience

Obedience is the power that unmasks evil's deceit. Obedience is the only path that can take us to true joy. Jesus knew it, he demonstrated it, and he taught it: "If you obey my commands, you will remain in my love, just as I have obeyed my Father's commands and remain in his love" (John 15:10).

Christ pointed to his own obedient walk as proof that the path of obedience leads to happiness. "If you want what I have," he said, in effect, "then walk as I have walked." Since his youth, Jesus was willing to be the son in whom the Father was "well pleased" (Mark 1:11). The Hebrew writer recorded that "although he was a son, he learned obedience" (Hebrews 5:8). He did as he was told, and joy was the result.

Lest anyone think that Jesus' joy came from his being King of the universe, note how he repeatedly described himself in a position of submission to the Father: "The Son can do nothing by himself; he can do only what he sees his Father doing" (John 5:19). He lived so that the source of his joy would be clear. It was through his submission, through his obedience, that happiness came. No stronger case for this can be made than the one found in Hebrews 12.

As the writer encouraged the Hebrew Christians to maintain their faith in Christ, he pointed to Jesus on the cross as the supreme example of steadfast devotion during a time of trial. Note the startling word he used: "Let us fix our eyes on Jesus, the author and perfecter of our faith, who for the *joy* set before him endured the cross, scorning its shame" (Hebrews 12:2).

Who would have thought that it was for joy that Christ went to the cross? Those painful crossbars seem to be the antithesis of happiness, yet Christ knew that the easier path of disobedience would never bring him bliss. As hymn writer Ray Overholt mused, "He could have called ten thousand angels." Christ knew that those angels could offer him momentary relief but that they could never give him eternal joy. Nothing short of steadfast obedience could yield true joy.

And there are modern examples of people who have proved that joy comes through obedience as well. Consider the athlete who obeys the coach's orders to be on the field before dawn. He or she knows that the agony of those laps is the passport to the joy of victory. The doctor who researches and toils into the night knows that true joy is not found in quitting when the going gets tough. The mother who dedicates the best years of her life to the nurture and rearing of her children knows that the joy she longs for cannot be found in shirking her duties. Obedience in life leads to the real treasures of joy.

Spiritual joy is no different. It is found in the loving obedience our Lord demands. Make no mistake, we do not earn heaven through our obedience. Grace is the only key that unlocks heaven's door, but joy comes as the by-product of loving God and keeping his commands. Joy is the result of a relationship that is based on voluntary submission to holy demands. As we bow to God's loving orders, he graciously crowns our lives with joy. This movement from obedience motivated by "have to" to obedience motivated by "want to" is the secret Christ gave his disciples at the table during that last night. Voluntary obedience to God is the sole route to true happiness.

Irish author Jim McGuiggan described well the happiness that one young man found as a result of obedience. Johnny loved to play basketball. To him, no finer night could be spent than one on the court. When his father asked him to miss a night at the gym to eat with a new family from down the street, he became upset. "Dad, do I have to?" he whined. His pleas were to no avail. He called his mates and gave his regrets. They extended their condolences.

Upon meeting the family, he was introduced to Mary, their lovely daughter who was just a few months younger than he was. They exchanged shy smiles at dinner. As the evening wore on, he grew bold enough to ask her for a dinner date of their own the following week. One dinner led to another, and soon Johnny and Mary were inseparable. When one of his old friends called and invited him to a night of hoops at the gym, Johnny respectfully declined. He had a date with Mary.

His buddy laughed and thought, *Poor chap! He's a slave to her now. Wasting a perfectly good evening with her when he could be down here playing ball with us!*

As Johnny hung up the phone, he smiled and thought, *Poor chaps! Running around for hours sweating in a smelly gym while I'll be out with my beautiful Mary.*

Jesus' words stand just as true today as they did during that last night with his disciples: "If you obey my commands, you will remain in my love.... I have told you this so that my joy may be in you and that your joy may be complete" (John 15:10–11). Only when we make the sacrifice of obedience do we discover the joy it holds.

SECTION THREE
WORDS OF ENCOURAGEMENT

The dinner was over twenty years ago, but I'll never forget the conversation. My college friend and I were playing an innocent parlor-game over Mexican food. Letting her start, I said, "Give me three words that people use to describe me."

Her barrage of unpleasant adjectives caught me off guard: "You're pushy, insensitive, uncaring, domineering, overbearing—"

"Enough already, I get the point!" I said with a laugh, but it was too late. For the next thirty minutes, I listened to a speech I needed but didn't desire. Though slightly overblown, her observations were fairly accurate.

I was ready to hand over my driver's license and resign from the human race when she paused and said, "And there's one more thing you need to know: I really love you."

"Did you say you love me?" I asked in shock.

"Yeah. Would I tell you all this if I didn't?" she asked with a grin. "I love you. Now, finish your tacos."

Those words were the encouragement I needed to deal with my faults. And I think Jesus would have approved, for after his strong words, he gave his disciples the encouraging words they needed:

> "You've got a friend."
> "You've been chosen."
> "If you need something, just ask."

For those who don't live in a world "where never is heard a discouraging word," here is the encouragement you've been waiting for. So finish your tacos, and let's dig into the good stuff.

Greater love has no one than this, that he lay down his life for his friends. You are my friends if you do what I command. I no longer call you servants, because a servant does not know his master's business. Instead, I have called you friends, for everything that I learned from my Father I have made known to you.

John 15:13–15

7

YOU'VE GOT A FRIEND

Who is Jesus to you? If this seems like an easy question to answer, try checking the box below that best describes your relationship to Him.

The best way to describe Jesus is to say that he is...

❑ My Lord

❑ My Savior

❑ My Shepherd

❑ My God

❑ My Buddy

If you chose one of the first four, you stand with the majority of Christians worldwide. Typically, our concept of Jesus has focused either on his power and authority or his divine mercy and guidance. He is lofty; we are lowly. He is the Good Shepherd; we are the naughty sheep. So didn't the last choice offered seem just a tad out of place? Doesn't thinking of Jesus as our "Buddy" seem a bit irreverent? I bet the disciples would have thought so too. That is, until the moment in the upper room when Jesus shocked them by calling them his "friends." "You are my friends," he said, "if you do what I command. I no longer call you servants, because a servant does not know his master's business. Instead, I have called you *friends*" (John 15:14–15).

Think of it. The son of God wants us—his followers—to think of him as a friend. An amigo. A pal. A chum. It's a pretty heady concept that could leave us with an inflated self-image. *Don't mess with me. I've got a friend in high places.* But that is exactly the kind of confidence our Lord wanted to inspire. Knowing how the world would accuse us and the devil would mock us, Jesus wanted us to feel secure in our relationship with him. So he called us *friends.*

Let it sink in for a minute: Jesus views you and me as personal friends.

We've all listened to folks use the words "personal friend" to brag about being buddies with a senator, hotshot actor, or corporate mogul. Claiming such a friendship gives them a sense of importance. It makes them feel big. If the truth be known, any of us who have known a famous person enjoy telling others about it. Okay, okay. If you insist, I'll tell you about my famous buddy, John Lovitz. John is the actor from *Saturday Night Live* who starred in *City Slickers II* and several commercials for the Yellow Pages. He has even participated in the award ceremony for the Oscars. But before all that, he lived in my dorm at college, and we were in several plays together. Has he called me recently? Well, no. But he's a friend!

Please understand, that's not what the Lord meant when he called you and me his friends. He wasn't just signifying that he could pick us out of a lineup on a church pew or that he once bumped into you in a baptistery. He was describing a much deeper, more meaningful relationship. He was assuring us that he is on our side, that he is a friend who will stand up for us.

John returned to this theme in his first epistle when he described Jesus as our advocate (1 John 2:1). Using legal language, John described a courtroom scene that has a bizarre twist. Imagine that we walk into court to face the Judge of all people. Our accuser is Satan, who sits at the prosecution table and objects to our every thought as being unworthy and unholy.

The Judge thunders, "How will you answer these charges?"

We squirm. We look around for our defense team, but nobody's there. So we reply, "We don't have a lawyer, your Honor."

"Then the court will appoint one," the Judge responds with a smile. With that, he steps down from the judge's bench, takes off his robes of authority, and takes a seat beside us!

Holding out a nail-pierced hand, he says, "My name is Jesus. I'm your new best friend."

But our friendship with Jesus doesn't happen automatically. It must grow and mature like any relationship. Jesus let the disciples in the upper room know this. He made it clear that they had crossed into a new level of relationship with him. Earlier that night, he had addressed them as "my children," but now he invited them to enter a different, deeper relationship. "I no longer call you servants," he said. "Instead, I have called you friends." Any parent who has watched his or her child go from being "my child" to "my friend" can understand how challenging that transition can be.

I used to be chained to the bunny slopes when my son Taylor and I went skiing. I helped him learn to turn safely and guarded against any wild-eyed snowboarders who might plow him under the powder. As Taylor's skiing ability grew, the tables quickly turned. During a recent, youth-group skiing trip, I found out just how far that table had turned. After a long day of skiing, we stood together at the top of a steep, icy slope. It was late afternoon, and my legs were talking to me. *You really think you can make it down this hill without breaking both of us?* they silently warned. Taylor must have spotted the worry in my eyes because he said, "Dad, you don't have to do this run if you don't feel like it. There's an easier way down over there. I'll wait for you at the bottom."

Something had changed between us since Taylor's days on the beginner slopes. He wasn't speaking to me as my son. He was talking to me as a friend. It gave me a strange feeling, nearly as strange as realizing that Jesus calls me his friend. When I struggle, he says, "Jeff, don't bite off more than you can chew, my friend. Let me fight this battle for you. I'm right here, pal."

But how does one develop this wonderful camaraderie with Jesus? How do we keep it from slipping away once it is established? As always, the words of Christ reveal the solution. Tucked into the teachings that Jesus offered his disciples at the table are four aspects of divine friendship, more of the truths he wanted every believer to know.

1. $\mathcal{F}$riendship Is Born out of Freedom

"Go make friends." How many kindergartners have been sent off on the first day of school with that instruction? And surprisingly, most do just that. They come back that afternoon talking confidently about sharing half a graham cracker with their new "best friend." But as we grow older, building the complex relationships we call friendships becomes less and less like making microwave popcorn and more and more like making a seven-layer wedding cake from scratch. Friendship is born out of freedom and can't be forced.

Parents who have agonized over their children's choice of companions know this. We only wish we could take our children to school and pick their friends for them. "That boy looks intelligent and pleasant. Why don't you be his friend?" "See that one with the ring through his lip? Steer clear of him!" But as in Shakespeare's famous play when the parents tried to pull Romeo from Juliet, they find that the heart of true friendship is free choice. So it is with Christ. He always offers his friendship freely. When he called the disciples *friends,* for example, he was under no obligation to do so, and they were under no obligation to accept. He did not force anyone into friendship, even when he wanted to: "O Jerusalem, Jerusalem...how often I have longed to gather your children together, as a hen gathers her chicks under her wings, but you were not willing" (Matthew 23:37). He desires that we choose him as freely as he chose us.

Remember, freedom in Christ is friendship with Christ. Take away that freedom to choose, and you are left with friendship by obligation—misery at best and slavery at worst. When obligation becomes the root of our faith, the friendship factor is lost. We then find ourselves going to church because of guilt and sitting through times of praise with one eye on the clock. We erect laws and demands to keep the Christian community in tow and ultimately lose all sense of free choice.

This was the pit the Pharisees fell into. This group of dedicated law keepers believed that the path to righteousness was reached through better laws. If the law said, "Don't touch a leper," they would say, "Don't let a leper's shadow fall on you." Loving God was boiled down to keeping commands. And when commands are the heart of a relationship, the relationship has lost its heart.

The maze of laws the Pharisees followed caused them to lose the sense of being a friend of God, as Abraham was called (James 2:23). It reduced them to being tenants who faithfully paid the rent or workers who met the day's quotas. That's why Christ's parable of the workers was so threatening to them (Matthew 20:1–16). In it, he described a manager who gave a full day's wages to workers who had only worked a few hours. That kind of gracious giving was incomprehensible to people who believed that you should only receive what you have earned. But not to our God. He chooses daily to give away blessings, not based on merit, but because we are his friends.

Our human friendships should teach us this as well. When a

good friend forgets his wallet and needs you to cover the check at lunch, you don't start the interest meter ticking the moment you pay the bill. And if he forgets to pay you back for two weeks, you won't send an invoice with ten percent added for late payment. In fact, when your friend does pay you back, you'll probably smile and say, "Oh, you didn't have to do that." But I'll bet you've never heard those words when you pay your Visa bill. Of course not. A creditor has the right to hold you to your word and make you pay your debt.

What a joyful surprise it is to know that our heavenly creditor chooses to treat us like close friends! When God forgives us through Christ, he does it out of his free will, not because of a contractual commitment. He knew we would forget to repay him when we "borrowed the money." In fact, he knew we would come back flat broke and say, "I'm sorry," once again. But rather than have our bad debt spoil our friendship, Jesus wipes it away, saying, in effect, "Have you forgotten? We are friends!"

2. Friendship Is Built through Communication

Think for a moment about your most valued friendships. What bonds you and your closest friend together? What forges the inner union you cherish?

It's not the hobbies you share, the experiences you enjoy, or even the values you have in common that forge a deep friendship. There are, for example, many folks who share my views whom I would hardly consider to be friends. On the contrary, there are people with whom I disagree strongly who are dear friends of mine. What is the difference? It is the closeness we have developed through the open and honest ways in which we share our thoughts.

True friendship grows through open communication. Just listen to the way we describe special friends: "I can tell him anything"; "There's nothing I couldn't talk about with her." In fact, the closeness of a relationship can be measured by the depth of honesty we share. As Ralph Waldo Emerson put it, a friend is "a person with whom I may think aloud."

Consider, for example, the kinds of facts that you tell a stranger: "Hello, my name is Jeff." But then, note the kinds of things that you tell an acquaintance: "My father died when I was twenty-one." Finally, there are the kinds of things that you tell only a close friend: "When my father died, I hurt so badly that…" The difference in the communication is obvious.

What may not be obvious is that our relationship with Christ is built on that same principle. Listen as Jesus described for the disciples the distinction between slaves and friends: "I no longer call you servants, because a servant does not know his master's business. Instead, I have called you friends, for everything that I learned from my Father I have made known to you" (John 15:15).

Jesus revealed himself to the disciples because he wanted to communicate with them as friends. He chose to pull back the curtain on his thoughts and motives and let them fully *know* him. And he does the same for us. What an amazing truth: We have been allowed to *know* God. That deserves pondering.

When I counsel couples whose relationships have fallen on hard times, one partner will often say, "I just don't feel like I really know him [or her] anymore." The power of that simple phrase is surprising because it can spell the end of a marriage or a friendship. Without that closeness, that intimate soul knowledge, there can be no trust, no love, and no true friendship. On the other hand, when two people really "know" each other, there is no storm they can't weather. Maybe that's why Jesus used those very words as he wept and cried out to God in the garden of Gethsemane.

In the middle of that emotional hurricane, he prayed the most succinct definition of salvation ever worded: "Now this is eternal life: that they may *know you,* the only true God, and Jesus Christ, whom you have sent" (John 17:3). There it is. The entirety of our struggles in life and God's plan for our fulfillment in two words: Know God. Isn't that what he was pointing the disciples toward when he called them his "friends"? And isn't that what he is saying to us today? "I want you to know me. I've held nothing back from you. There is no door I would not open to you. You need not be worried about any surprises or any sudden changes on my part: You know me too well for that!"

But divine friendship is a two-way street. Christ not only wants to reveal his nature to us, he asks us to open our hearts to him. Through the avenue of prayer, he wants us to express the depths of our fears and failings to the Father. "Cast all your anxiety on him," Scripture invites, "because he cares for you" (1 Peter 5:7). If we really believe in our friendship with Christ, no subject will be too personal to explore, no problem too painful to discuss.

A Christian friend recently brought up this very issue when he asked, "What can I do to deepen my prayer life?" He felt as if he wasn't praying often enough or long enough. But more important, he was frustrated by his lack of desire to pray. He was looking for good books or tapes on prayer when I sidetracked him. "Maybe prayer isn't your problem," I suggested.

He looked at me like I was a few feathers short of a duck. "But of course, prayer is my problem!"

"Really?" I asked. "If you weren't talking enough with your wife, would you think the problem was your mouth? You wouldn't go to the dentist and ask him to examine your teeth. You would go to a counselor and ask him to examine your relationship!"

It is no different with Jesus. Our prayer life has a direct connection to our friendship with Christ. The less we pray, the colder the relationship grows and the less we want to pray. So if we want to rejuvenate our prayer life, then it may be time to reexamine our friendship with our Lord. If we truly trust the divine friendship he offers us, we should be dying to talk with him.

Traveling salespeople and other "road warriors" understand this principle. When you've been away on business for a week and are lying on the bed in a lonely motel room, your thoughts wander to what's going on back at home. *It's 8:30,* you think. *The kids are just getting into bed. Mom is reading the little ones a story or saying prayers with the oldest one. Soon she'll go into our bedroom and browse the newspaper.* If you think about it for another minute, what will you do? You won't want to turn on the television or read a book. You want to be home, so you reach for the next best thing to being there and pick up the phone. Before you know it, you've spent an hour on the phone chatting with your wife about everything and nothing. You talk about the day's events, you tell her how you long to be with her, and you plan what you'll do when you're together again. You sound just like you did when you were first dating! And you sound just like David when he talked with God: "On my bed I remember you; I think of you through the watches of the night. Because you are my help, I sing in the shadow of your wings. My soul clings to you; your right hand upholds me" (Psalm 63:6–8).

If we accept Jesus' assurance that we can know him and trust him like our best friend, we will be more prone to have deep, long conversations in prayer with him. And as our relationship with him grows, we will be ready for the ultimate step in a committed friendship. We will be ready to sacrifice for our friend.

3. Friendship Is Based on Sacrifice

True friendship costs! That truth has been proven through time. Four hundred years before Christ, the ancient Greek Euripides wrote, "Friends—and I mean real friends—reserve nothing; the property of one belongs to the other." Jesus took friendship to an even deeper level when he said, "Greater love has no one than this, that he lay down his life for his friends" (John 15:13).

Most of us will never experience the ultimate test of friendship: sacrificing our lives for other people. But a little blue dot on the back of my driver's license helped me to get a better picture of what Christ was saying. That dot designates me as an organ donor. In the event of a catastrophic accident, I have agreed to have the usable parts of my body "harvested" for others. When I agreed to the program, I never asked to whom my organs would be donated. There are no stipulations that the recipient has to be a Christian or even a country music fan. After all, if I'm dead, what difference would it make?

But what if the government suddenly changed the rules to allow organs to be taken whenever they were needed, even if the donor is still alive? Officials could then come asking for my kidney or my liver while I'm still using them. If I protest, they could say, "Hey, you agreed to be a donor. We need those organs now, if you don't mind."

So now what would I do? Although I would love to say that I would give up a vital part of my body for a total stranger, I can't make that pledge. Before anyone placed me on the operating table, I'd have to know who needed my body parts—and why! And I would make my decision about giving them up based on the answer. I'm not turning my spleen over to just anybody. It would have to be a pretty close friend, don't you think?

Now look up at the cross. What a pledge of friendship it symbolizes. Jesus freely donated his heart—his life—for you. He was willing to give up heaven and take up the cross because of his love for us. It was the ultimate proof of friendship that we needed in order to get through the long days of waiting for his return. And it is the ultimate sign of his love that we needed in order to motivate us to sacrifice in return.

Because friendship is a mutual agreement, we must be willing to make sacrifices for him too. Whether we wash dirty feet as he did in the upper room or forgive those who have wronged us as he did on the cross, our friendship with Christ is based on his sacrifice but must continue through our sacrifices. We can never match his gracious gift, but we must be always ready to do whatever our "holy friend" asks. That's why we must add one final element to our understanding of this friendship.

4. Friendship Is Preserved through Accountability

The simple message, "Friends don't let friends drive drunk," was the key to the most successful advertising campaign ever waged in the war against drunk driving. Some observers suggest that it worked so well because it appealed not to the drunk driver but to his or her more sober friends. I suspect it worked because it appealed to the power of friendship. Friendship says, "If I care about you, I won't stand by and watch you hurt yourself."

It is in that context that we must understand the last statement that Christ gave concerning our divine friendship: "You are my friends if you do what I command" (John 15:14). This verse has derailed plenty of believers, causing many of them to worry that Jesus offers a tenuous and fickle friendship. They translate these words to mean, "If you do as I say, I'll be your friend. If you don't, forget it!" But Jesus' very actions deny that meaning. He sacrificed his life for us without regard to our obedience.

The Bible proclaims this truth in Romans 5:8. "God demonstrates his own love for us in this: While we were still sinners, Christ died for us." We are forgiven because of our faith in him, not our faithful performance. Our salvation is built on his work, not ours. So what, then, did Christ mean when he said, "If you do what I command"?

Rather than pulling the rug out from under our assurance, Jesus was affirming the nature of our relationship with him. He was saying, in effect, "Friends don't let friends ignore God." When we become friends of Christ, we trust his advice and want to follow it. He, in turn, calls us to obedience because the nature of our relationship with him demands it. As author and speaker Max Lucado says so well, "God loves you just like you are, but he loves you too much to leave you that way." Jesus could no more ignore our sin than we could stand back and watch one of our children drink poison. It is because we are his friends that he wants us to obey his commands. And it is because we are his friends that we want to obey.

This commitment to godly obedience should also be reflected in the way in which we care for one another. Christian friends don't let Christian friends ignore God. Although each of us is independent and free before God, as Christians we are also a part of his holy family. That relationship prompts us to care about our brothers' and sisters' choices and to encourage them to do what is right. If we don't, what kind of friends are we?

A memory from a Sunday gone by makes the point well. I had just reached that magic age, nine years old, at which my mother allowed me to sit with my friends during church. The youth group always sat in the front section of pews, and my mom sat in the back. Although it was glorious not having her within "pinching range," ready to correct my every move, my newfound freedom quickly went to my head. I started passing notes and joking with a fellow next to me until the young lady on my right nudged me hard enough to break a rib. Before I could say a word, she motioned to the end of the pew. There stood the most frightening sight I could have seen during a worship assembly: my mother. She had walked all the way from the back of the church to the row in which I was seated in order to correct me.

Actually, my mother had not come just to correct me. She had come to "collect" me, to take me directly out to the lobby—the dreaded "or else" that Mom had always threatened when I misbehaved in church. "Do you want me to have to take you out?" she used to whisper.

I tried to look innocent, giving her that "Who me, warden?" look that children can do so well. But she was not to be swayed. She motioned with one finger for me to come to her, and when I got within pinching range the punishment began. She grabbed my ear and squeezed it with all her might as she walked me up the aisle of the church. That aisle had never seemed so long! By the time we reached the back of the church, every member had noticed us. Even my father paused during his sermon and nodded gravely at us as if to say, "Whack him one for me, Ma." Once we entered the lobby, my mother took me to a private corner and gave me what for—and then some.

When church concluded, I was forced to stand with my father while he shook hands and to wait for whatever additional punishment he thought proper. While I rubbed my sore backside and contemplated my dim future, someone tapped me on the shoulder. It was my good friend Brad. "Your mother really nailed you, huh?"

"She sure did!" I sniffled out.

"You know, she tried to get your attention for half an hour before she came down there," he said with a smirk.

"How do you know that?"

"Because I saw her, dummy!"

My cheeks began to flush anew. Brad had been sitting right behind me during the whole service. "Why didn't you tell me to knock it off?" I demanded.

The strangest look came over his face. It was clear that the notion of correcting me had never occurred to him. Finally he said, "Hey man, I'm not your mother."

I nearly decked him right there in the church lobby.

Jesus has called us friends, but he calls on us to be friends as well. As we delight in his friendship, as we build on that relationship through time in study and prayer, and as we stand in awe of the sacrifice he made to make it happen, let us also commit to being for one another the kind of friend that Jesus is to us.

It's one more of the truths he wanted us to know and obey until he returns.

I no longer call you servants, because a servant does not know his master's business. Instead, I have called you friends, for everything that I learned from my Father I have made known to you. You did not choose me, but I chose you and appointed you to go and bear fruit—fruit that will last. Then the Father will give you whatever you ask in my name.

John 15:15–16

8

YOU'VE BEEN CHOSEN

I live across the street from an Oscar addict. She'll admit it—just ask her. She plans her schedule for the month of March around the night they announce the winners of the Oscars during the Academy Awards television show. The Oscars are the film world's equivalent to the Super Bowl rings of football. Taking home one of those gold statuettes can change a person's life forever. So along with millions of other people, our neighbor prepares for Oscar night like a U.S. marine preparing for battle. She buys the special edition of *People Weekly* that covers the nominees. She makes her own list of winners before the show. She'll try to have seen all the movies nominated so she can be ready to respond when they say, "And the award goes to..." She places her favorite snacks by her side and puts the kids to bed early. Then she settles into her favorite chair and waits for the show to begin.

Last year, my wife and I got to watch the Academy Awards show with our neighbor and her husband. It was quite an experience. When the judges chose an actor our neighbor didn't approve of or a film that she felt was undeserving, she booed the television screen. Being a movie buff myself, I got swept along in the action pretty quickly. I started booing and cheering with her. Soon the four of us were weighing in on the stupidity of the judges or the brilliance of their choices. We had a blast being movie critics for a night.

Some of our responses reminded me of how I imagine the angels must have reacted when God announced his choices for the award of eternal life. Surely they must have been shocked when he proclaimed, "And the gift of eternal life goes to…humans!" Didn't their jaws drop and their wings fall silent when God chose to send his Son to die for the sins of humanity? Heaven must have been filled with cries of "I can't believe it!" and "They don't deserve it." But it was too late for second-guessing. God had chosen to save the human race through Jesus Christ, and nothing would ever be the same.

It is the amazing truth of God's choice to save us that Jesus was moved to emphasize during the Last Supper. There, he reminded the apostles of how they were invited to that august circle. "You did not choose me," he said, "but I chose you" (John 15:16). In the middle of his beautiful words about friendship, Jesus let them know that they weren't gathered around that table just because of their good looks or faithful service; they had been chosen.

Surely this fact was no shock to the Twelve. Each knew that he had been called by Christ from his fishing nets or tax tables to be a part of this inner circle, this chosen few. Admittedly, they might not have known the enormity of that choice. They had no idea that their names would be memorized by millions and etched in stone in countless chapels for years to come. But surely none of them thought they had chosen Jesus. They knew they had not picked him to be their Messiah.

Or had they? After three years of following Jesus, perhaps they each had arrived at the same faulty conclusion we often do: *I'm a Christian because I'm a good guy. I chose to turn from the world and follow Christ of my own free will. Isn't my church fortunate to have me? Isn't God lucky I chose him?*

But what is the truth? Did we choose God, or did He choose us? The question is not easily answered, but it is one with which every believer must wrestle. If Jesus thought it was important enough to mention in his final preparation lesson before the cross, we can't just dismiss it as unsolvable or irrelevant. What we can do is see the two sides of this important concept and learn to appreciate the blessings that they bring. To do so, we must understand two foundational truths: God's sovereign choice and our free will.

God's Sovereign Choice

One of my son's favorite riddles used to be, "Where does a five-hundred-pound canary make its nest?" The answer, of course, is, "Anywhere it wants to."

The same can be said of the sovereignty of God. There is nothing that runs outside his influence. There is no force outside his control. From the spinning planets of the solar system to the whirling atoms within us, God directs the course of every one. He is the one who makes his rest "anywhere he wants to." Listen to a portion of his discourse with Job: "Who shut up the sea behind doors when it burst forth from the womb...when I said, 'This far you may come and no farther; here is where your proud waves halt'?" (Job 38:8, 11).

God's authority is unlimited. His knowledge is without bounds. His power is unmeasured. That's why we call him the Almighty. I love A. W. Tozer's description of God's sovereignty: "Can we imagine the Lord God of Hosts having to request permission of anyone or to apply for anything to a higher body? To whom would God go for permission? Who is higher than the Highest? Who is mightier than the Almighty?"

God's active role in the history of our world should leave no doubt regarding his supremacy or his divinity. I doubt that anyone who was standing at the foot of Mount Sinai when Moses went up to receive the Ten Commandments questioned God's authority. I don't think anyone who saw the thunder and lightning cover its peak turned to a nearby person and asked, "You think God is really all-powerful?"

But his powerful, past actions should also convince us that he has the ability to choose our destinies today as well. The writer of Ecclesiastes reminds us, "When times are good, be happy; but when times are bad, consider: God has made the one as well as the other" (Ecclesiastes 7:14).

God's ability to control our destinies is not a notion with which modern people are completely comfortable. We are raised with the belief that we hold the reins of our future. To our way of thinking, God may decide where hurricanes or tornadoes occur, but *we* are in charge of our careers and dreams. *We* are the masters of our destinies. Through hard work and ingenuity we can forge our *own* futures. But before we go too far down that road, we ought to consider the story of Jacob and Esau as told by Paul in Romans. It throws a huge wrench into the gears of our independent logic.

Esau and Jacob were the first twins recorded in Scripture, and from the very beginning they were in competition. The Bible even says that they came out of the womb fighting for position, with Jacob the younger clinging to the heel of Esau. Years later, through trickery and deceit, Jacob stole his older brother's birthright and took the premier place he had wanted for so long. Their story may appear to be nothing more than a severe case of sibling rivalry, but Paul lets us in on a little secret: God had the whole thing planned out ahead! Paul wrote, "Yet, before the twins were born or had done anything good or bad—in order that God's purpose in election might stand: not by works but by him who calls—she [Rebekah, their mother] was told, 'The older will serve the younger.' Just as it is written: 'Jacob I loved, but Esau I hated'" (Romans 9:11–13).

Jacob triumphed over his brother, not because he was smarter or slicker, but because God wanted it that way! God *chose* Jacob. Paul emphasized God's choice in the matter by asking, "What then shall we say? Is God unjust? Not at all! For he says to Moses, 'I will have mercy on whom I have mercy, and I will have compassion on whom I have compassion'" (Romans 9:14–15).

If a voice inside you is saying, "That's not fair!" then welcome to the party. Our contemporary notion of fairness feels crushed before the steamroller of God's power. We think, *How can God pick one person over the other like that? It's not right. It's not fair! It's not equal opportunity under the law!* But before you call your lawyer to sue Jehovah for unfair practices, know that God's sovereignty is not diminished by our difficulty in accepting or understanding it. He is God—with or without our permission. Half of our battle is getting over that one fact.

One cannot look very far through Scripture without being confronted by God's sovereign choices again and again. God chose Jacob, Moses, and David for their appointed places. He picked Mary to be Christ's mother and Joseph to be Christ's earthly father. Jesus chose the twelve apostles to be his initial emissaries of the good news. He selected them by his own wisdom, without consulting an employment agency. If he had done background checks, I'm sure a few of his chosen ones would never have made the cut. But no matter what their strengths or weaknesses, they were his chosen twelve.

And the disciples aren't the only ones Jesus chose. One of my favorite passages of Scripture has long been Romans 8:28, which begins, "And we know that in all things God works for the good of those who love him." I used to quote that part whenever life's circumstances went sour. When I studied the rest of the verse, however, I found I was quoting a much deeper theology than I understood.

Consider what follows: "...who *have been called* according to his purpose" (Romans 8:28).

As Christians, you and I also were called and chosen by God to be his people. We are part of his grand purpose. We were called to receive salvation. In fact, we received the gift of eternal life only because he chose to give it to us. It is not by chance that we are called "God's chosen people." As Paul reminded his readers, "In him we were also chosen, having been predestined according to the plan of him who works out everything in conformity with the purpose of his will" (Ephesians 1:11).

But these Scriptures do not stand alone. They lead us to a second truth we must understand, one that seems to stand in contradiction to all we have just read. That second truth is this: God chose to give us free will.

*O*ur Free Choice

The story of mankind's first sin carries many foundational precepts, but none is more important or evident than the reality of our free will. God placed Adam and Eve in the garden and allowed them to choose between good and evil. God neither forced them to do good nor made them commit sin. He simply set them free to choose, and they chose sin. God punished them, but in his mercy God also gave them another chance. He allowed them to choose again.

Over and over in the Old Testament's record of human history, the cycle was repeated. Sometimes people chose to follow God and were blessed, sometimes they chose to ignore him and were punished. Repeatedly, God's people were encouraged to choose righteousness. Joshua's final speech to them is a classic example of this encouragement: "Now fear the LORD and serve him with all faithfulness. Throw away the gods your forefathers worshiped beyond the River and in Egypt, and serve the LORD. But if serving the LORD seems undesirable to you, then *choose* for yourselves this day whom you will serve.... But as for me and my household, we will serve the LORD" (Joshua 24:14–15).

Joshua wanted the Israelites to know that they had to make a choice, the same choice standing before us. Whom will we serve? Only we can choose our master. The New Testament echoes the theme of personal choice repeatedly:

> But *seek* first his kingdom and his righteousness, and all these things will be given to you as well. (Matthew 6:33)

> Therefore do not let sin reign in your mortal body so that you obey its evil desires. Do not offer the parts of your body to sin, as instruments of wickedness, but rather *offer yourselves* to God. (Romans 6:12–13)

> *Set your minds* on things above, not on earthly things. (Colossians 3:2)

> We know that we have come to know him *if we obey* his commands. (1 John 2:3)

Every admonishment to obey, to seek righteousness, or to follow

God's will is an affirmation of our ability to choose. If we were unable to choose, why would God tell us to do so? If we have no free will and God does not want "anyone to perish," as the Bible says (2 Peter 3:9), then everyone on earth would be a follower of Christ! But one look around tells us how untrue this is.

On the contrary, God calls us to follow him because he knows that we can choose not to. He makes provision for us to return to him when we have wandered away because we will often choose to wander. He calls to us like sheep, and he will not drag us into his will like wayward chicks. *We must choose his will.* As author James Dobson has said, "God gave us a free choice because there is no significance to love that knows no alternative."

Furthermore, even after we have chosen Christ we have the ability to renounce our choice. Although the doctrine of "once saved, always saved" is an attractive one, we can choose to leave the security of God's hand. Scripture speaks of the sad case of those who have forsaken their "first love" (Revelation 2:4) or who have "shipwrecked their faith" (1 Timothy 1:19). They willfully chose to walk away from God. To say it more bluntly, hell is always an option if we want to choose it. This is why the apostle Paul was so arduous in his quest to keep choosing to follow God. He knew the "other choice" was ever lurking nearby, waiting for him to glance its way. But he was determined to stick by his Lord. "No, I beat my body and make it my slave," he wrote, "so that after I have preached to others, I myself will not be disqualified for the prize" (1 Corinthians 9:27).

CHAPTER 8

$\mathcal{L}$iving with Both Choices

If, then, we serve an almighty God who controls everything, how can it be that we are free to choose to obey or to disregard him? Any answer that diminishes God's power or our free choice is faulty, and I've never read an answer that doesn't do one or the other. The hard truth is, both God's sovereignty and our free choice exist side by side in Scripture. God allows us to choose, yet he reserves his ultimate ability to judge. We are free to choose our own path, but God can chart our course as he sees fit.

It is confusing to consider that God's omnipotence and sovereignty make him responsible for every tragic loss in the world. It is frustrating to contemplate that our choices are allowed only by his choice. It is mentally exhausting to try to bring his sovereignty and our free will into logical harmony.

But don't let these theological complexities mask the really important decisions. These mental puzzles are mere academic debate when compared with the challenge of living daily for Jesus. It is the practical decisions like which television shows we choose to watch or how faithful we choose to be to our respective spouses that will make the difference. The truth is that fighting to fathom the divine will of God in matters we can't understand can keep us from faithfully making the simple, daily choices we completely understand. At times, we need to be reminded that we are not privy to the back rooms of heaven and that God has not invited us to his divine planning meetings. Instead, he reveals our lives one day at a time, one choice at a time. Like children peering at a parade through a hole in the fence, we see only the part of life that is in front of us at the moment. Trying to comprehend the whole scenario from our limited view is beyond our ability. Our challenge is to stay focused on doing our job…not on doing God's.

Jesus knew how difficult this would be for us. For that reason, he not only told the disciples that they were chosen, but he also told them why. He gave them purpose on which to focus. "I chose you and appointed you to go and bear fruit," he said, "fruit that will last" (John 15:16).

Jesus has chosen each of us purposefully. Not one of us was chosen by accident or happenstance. Although we were not selected in the same way as Peter, Andrew, James, or John, we have been called and chosen by our Savior. He has chosen us to share his light with a spiritually dark world, to be his people, his messengers, and his advocates on earth.

The only choice that remains is what we will do about his choice. It is the ultimate irony that we have the ability to choose to ignore God's choice. We can walk away from his open arms and spurn his holy invitation. We can turn down the divine Oscar he has chosen to give each of us. But why would anyone do that? The answer may be seen in the stories of two men who were paralyzed in tragic accidents.

One man was Kenneth Wright, a high-school football star who later became an avid wrestler, boxer, hunter, and skin diver. A broken neck sustained in a wrestling match in 1979 left him paralyzed from the chest down. He underwent therapy, and his doctors were hopeful that one day he would walk with the help of braces and crutches. But the former athlete apparently could not reconcile him-self to his physical condition. He prevailed upon two of his best friends to take him in his wheelchair to a wooded area and leave him alone with a twelve-gauge shotgun. After they left, he held the shot-gun to his abdomen and pulled the trigger. Kenneth Wright died at age twenty-four.

The second paraplegic is Jim McGowan. Thirty years ago, at the age of nineteen, he was stabbed and left paralyzed from the middle of his chest down. He is confined to a wheelchair, but he made the news recently when he made a successful parachute jump, landing on his target in the middle of Lake Wallenpaupack in the Poconos. Jim lives alone, cooks his meals, washes his clothes, and cleans his house. He drives himself in a specially equipped automobile. He has written three books, and he did the photography for our country's first book on the history of wheelchair sports.

What causes two similar lives to head toward such different des-tinations? About just such challenges, Oswald Chambers wrote, "These things either make us fiends or they make us saints. It depends entirely on the relationship we are in toward God." Indeed, our closeness to the King determines how we handle the circum-stances he creates. So when crises come, never forget that God saved you for a purpose. Don't let anything rob you of that security. Fulfill your purpose in Christ, and be prepared to accept your heavenly "Oscar." Your Father has cast the ballot, and the result is no secret: He *chose* you!

I will do whatever you ask in my name, so that the Son may bring glory to the Father. You may ask me for anything in my name, and I will do it. You did not choose me, but I chose you and appointed you to go and bear fruit—fruit that will last. Then the Father will give you whatever you ask in my name.

John 14:13–14; 15:16

9

IF YOU NEED IT,
JUST ASK

Margaret was dying, or so the doctors had said. A fast-growing type of cancer had been found in her lymphatic system. Those who've walked the halls of a cancer ward know that's not good news. The doctors prescribed chemotherapy and radiation as standard procedure, but their faces betrayed their lack of hope.

Margaret was dying, but her church didn't think it was time. You see, she was one of those older ladies whom other Christians just love. Faithful and gentle, she was an example to all of the ladies in the church. As a wife of one of the elders, she had endured with grace and humility the challenges that the limelight brings. She was always willing to serve—through teaching and leading or cooking and cleaning.

So the congregation began to pray for her. In large groups and small circles, her name was brought before God for weeks on end. The medical treatments continued, and she slowly began to weaken. The end was coming.

I clearly remember the telephone call I received from a fellow church member who asked, "Have you heard about Margaret?" I braced myself for bad news, but it wasn't bad at all. Margaret had just received a clean bill of health from her doctors! The cancer had disappeared! Even her doctors had to concede that this was the work of the Great Physician.

When someone asked her why she was healed, Margaret said with a smile, "Because we asked God for it!"

I cherish stories such as this, especially when they involve people I know personally, such as Margaret. But someone else may view this story from a very different perspective. "Why did God make her well? Why hasn't he done that for my loved one?" Questions such as these can take us to the dark side of our doubts, but they don't have to. Jesus offers a soft touch and a quiet answer to such difficult questions. It is the same message he offered to his disciples as he prepared to leave them: Keep asking. Not once, but three times during that evening he reminded them of the great privilege they enjoyed:

> I will do whatever you ask in my name, so that the Son may bring glory to the Father. You *may ask me for anything in my name, and I will do it.* (John 14:13–14)

> The Father will *give you whatever you ask in my name.* (John 15:16)

In that day you will no longer ask me anything. I tell you the truth, my Father will *give you whatever you ask in my name.* (John 16:23)

Up to this point, the disciples had turned to Jesus with their every need. Whether they were asking for bread to feed the five thousand or peace to help them face a stormy sea, Jesus was there to provide it. But things were about to change. Although Jesus would no longer be with them in the flesh, they needed to know that he would still meet their needs. So he promised them a "hot line" to heaven that would give them the power to call on God for anything they needed to complete their ministries.

The Book of Acts shows that they used this gift mightily. Through God's power, they healed the lame and caused the blind to see. They were set free from prison and were given ability to speak in languages they'd never studied. They worked miracles that stunned the crowds and stopped the mockers. In short, they asked—and God gave.

How do you feel when you read about the results of this apostolic blessing? Do you find yourself wishing you had that kind of communication with the Father? Do you feel as if you're standing out in the cold, looking into the warmth and wealth of someone else's home?

God knew that the apostles weren't the only ones who would need his help while waiting for Jesus to return. So he gave every believer assurances that sound strikingly similar to the words Jesus spoke to the apostles. Scattered throughout the New Testament are prayer promises such as these:

I tell you the truth.... If you believe, you will receive whatever you ask for in prayer. (Matthew 21:21–22)

If any of you lacks wisdom, he should ask God, who gives generously to all without finding fault, and it will be given to him. (James 1:5)

Dear friends…we have confidence before God and receive from him anything we ask. (1 John 3:21–22)

This is the confidence we have in approaching God: that if we ask anything according to his will, he hears us. And if we know that he hears us—whatever we ask—we know that we have what we asked of him. (1 John 5:14–15)

Holy batphone! Do you see all of these promises? The apostles weren't the only ones who could ask for what they needed. Jesus wants all believers to know that the Father stands ready to meet our needs as well. Through the power of prayer, we can ask God for blessings, and he has promised that we will receive all we need.

Don't let anyone tell you that prayer is an out-of-date check that expired somewhere around A.D. 70. God is just as alive today as ever. He is answering prayer and handing out blessings right here, right now.

But before we get out our laundry lists of wants, let's carefully examine what Jesus has told us about the privilege of prayer. Too many people have plunged into prayer while thinking of God as the great Coke machine in the sky. They put in their quarter-hour of prayer and expect the good stuff to drop out below! But that's not what Jesus meant, nor is it what even the apostles found. Indeed, Paul described times when God did not take away the "thorn" in his flesh or "open a door" of opportunity despite the apostle's pleas (2 Corinthians 12:7–9). It is clear that prayer is not a blank check from Jehovah. Prayer requires both the countersignature of Christ and the Father's stamp of agreement before it can be cashed.

So how do we access the great blessing that prayer brings? What should our expectations be regarding what we ask for and what we hope to receive from God? Jesus' words provide a path to the answers we need. Within his comments to the disciples, we can find four distinct principles that can shore up our faith in prayer without placing our expectations beyond Christ's intent.

1. *If* You Ask

After a lesson on sin and confession, a Sunday-school teacher asked her second-grade class, "What must we do before we can be forgiven?"

One bright-eyed boy blurted out, "You gotta sin!"

Although it sounds simplistic, the first principle Jesus reminded us of is no more complex than this child's response. Before we can expect God to provide us with the things we need, we gotta ask! The question is not, "Does God have the power to meet our needs?" Rather, it is, "Will we have the faith and presence of mind to ask?"

Unfortunately, the simplicity of prayer has led many people into complacency. It strikes them as too easy, too childish, just to bow their heads and recite their needs. These people want to exhaust their own resources before turning to God. "Wouldn't the time be better spent by doing something about the problem?" the modern thinker asks.

And Satan loves that kind of thinking. If he can keep us from turning to the Father with our needs, he can keep us frustrated and frantic. That scenario reminds me of the old Superman television show. Every plot led to virtually the same dilemma: Jimmy Olsen and Lois Lane would be captured by dastardly fiends who would leave them tied up in a basement. In that same basement, a huge bomb would be set to destroy the city in minutes. So the fiends would leave the two, hapless reporters to watch their last seconds of life tick away. For some reason known only to the writers of the show, the bad guys always forgot one little detail. They managed to leave Jimmy and Lois tied up in a room that had a phone! Once the two were alone, the race against time began. Would they get out of their bonds and call for help? Would they reach Superman in time?

Notice that the question is not, "Can Superman stop a bomb?" Any six-year-old knows that dynamite is no match for the Man of Steel. The only suspense is, "Will those two klutzes get to the phone in time?"

Our battle against Satan is no different. God's ability to meet our needs is never in question. He can change hearts and cure tumors. He has done it before, and he will do it again. David recognized this when he prayed, "In your hands are *strength* and *power* to exalt and give strength to all" (1 Chronicles 29:12). The only uncertainty is our unwillingness to ask.

Will we ask God for the things we need? The issue is not that

God doesn't know what we need. Our omniscient Lord knows our needs before we speak them. He has his angels ready to deliver the blessings we require, but he has decreed that the angels must wait for our requests.

In view of Christ's words, our motto should be, "Ask God first...then go do what you can!" He should be our source of first recourse, not our Hail Mary pass of last resort. But Jesus didn't stop here. He went on to offer even greater encouragement to pray.

2. *Whatever* You Ask

I heard a story about three preachers who were bragging at a conference about their prayer powers. The one from the East Coast said, "You know, when our church prays for healing, the patients get well about half the time."

The preacher from the Midwest replied, "Well, we pray for rain, and it happens about seventy percent of the time."

After a moment, the preacher from the West spoke up: "Well, at our church we have a sunrise prayer service, and it works every time."

Many of us ask God for only the simple or even predictable blessings of life. "Just get me through today, Lord," we pray. Or, "Keep me from harm during this trip." Requests such as these seem a little anemic when compared to the way Christ described the disciples' latitude in asking God for help. His language to the disciples was astonishingly broad. "*Whatever* you ask...," he said (John 14:13). The apostle John echoed this commitment in 1 John

5:14–15: "This is the confidence we have in approaching God: that if we ask anything according to his will, he hears us. And if we know that he hears us—whatever we ask—we know that we have what we asked of him."

This willingness of God to be so openhanded and gracious is an affront to our logic and a test of our faith. His generosity goes far beyond our typical, "give us this day our daily bread" requests. Yet Jesus repeated the promise three times for the disciples, each time using the all-encompassing words *whatever* and *anything*. His strong emphasis leaves us with the sense that God has much more to give than we are normally willing to ask. What a faith challenge that is!

Imagine the scene. We come into God's storehouse where every wondrous blessing of joy unknown and peace without limits is stored. The Lord has called the angels to attention, and they have prepared a huge chariot to transport the blessings his children will request. Twenty thousand of heaven's finest, fresh from the Heavenly Fitness Center, stand ready to do the heavy lifting and load our cargo. And for what will we ask? We look around longingly at all of these treasures and then quietly beg God for a small pack of dry crackers and a glass of water! The Father is appalled. The angels are dumbfounded. They give us the tiny things we request, and after we trudge out they ask the King, "What's wrong? Why do they pray such puny prayers?"

With a sad smile, he replies, "They have a hard time asking as big as I can give."

What a tragedy to realize that God has bigger things planned for us but we miss out on them because we simply won't ask for them.

God has shown us the immense power of his hand, and he has offered it to us if we will but ask. Perhaps we just listened too well to our mothers who, when we ate at someone else's home, warned, "If it's not on the table, don't ask for it." With all due respect to moms, God says, "Go ahead and ask!"

If you are worried about appearing too bold or presumptuous, take heart in the example of the patriarch Abraham, who repeatedly asked God to extend more mercy to the cities of Sodom and Gomorrah (see Genesis 18).

Although the eventual destruction of those cities often over-shadows this aspect of the story, Abraham's boldness is worth noting. No fewer than six times he asked God to extend more mercy. He "bargained" with God, appealing to his kindness to save the city for fifty righteous folks, and finally to save it for only ten. He asked God to hear his request with a candor and boldness that would have got-ten my mouth smacked at the dinner table: "Far be it from you," he said to God, "to do such a thing—to kill the righteous with the wicked, treating the righteous and the wicked alike. Far be it from you! Will not the Judge of all the earth do right?" (Genesis 18:25).

This kind of boldness is typical of God's heroes. Throughout the Old Testament and into the New Testament, we see that God's people were willing to ask for amazing things. At their requests, he stopped the sun, parted the sea, and raised the dead. When they prayed, he shook buildings, dropped walls, and destroyed armies. Just about the time we think we have hit the Lord's limit for giving, Paul reminds us that God "is able to do *immeasurably* more than all we ask or imagine" (Ephesians 3:20).

When you ask the King of the universe for something, don't be shy! Ask for something big! But as you do, make sure that you are asking in the right name.

3. *On* My Name

An interesting change happened as Jesus spoke to the disciples about his power during the Last Supper. Until that time, he had always told them to "ask the Father" when they had needs. But in preparation for his time away from them, he revealed his own authority and offered them the strength found in his holy name. "And *I will do* whatever you ask in my name, so that the Son may bring glory to the Father. You may ask me for anything *in my name, and I will do it*" (John 14:13–14).

Nothing less than equality with God was required to speak those words. The disciples must have held their breath when they heard such claims from someone who had walked with them for three years. But the shock was unavoidable. Jesus needed them to know that he was not just a prophet, not just a messenger, and not just a conveyer of requests to God. He needed them to know that when they spoke his name, they were dealing with the "Boss." Jesus had full authority to grant their requests, and he would do so…as long as they asked *in his name.*

Jesus' instruction to ask in his name is no minor addendum or holy fine print. In his day, a messenger would often come "in the name of" his lord or ruler. This meant that the message he carried was to be received as if it were given personally by that powerful person. If the messenger was mistreated, as in Jesus' parable of the unjust tenants, it was as if the cruel act had been done to the master himself. Furthermore, the messenger was to behave in a way befitting his master. If the messenger's actions were rude or inappropriate, he would bring shame on his master's name and punishment on himself.

Consider, then, how this instruction relates to our prayers. We are taught to ask in Jesus' name. Our requests, then, must be presented both with faith in our Master and in accordance with his nature. Prayers filled with selfish lists of "gimmes," for example, can hardly be offered in Jesus' holy name. Before intoning that precious and powerful phrase, we must be sure that the things for which we are asking will bring glory to his name.

Consider a common example. When we pray for a friend or relative to be healed, why do we do it? If it is simply so that we can enjoy more days with the person or so that we won't be hurt by the individual's death, we may be praying from what James calls "selfish ambition." If we ask God to heal so that his name will be glorified and his kingdom furthered, then we truly are asking "in his name."

Moses prayed in this manner when he appealed to God not to destroy the Israelites at the foot of Mount Sinai. Moses had just received the divine dictation we call the Ten Commandments, but while he was "in session" with God, the children of Israel started whining like babies. Ever ready to turn back to idolatry, they convinced Aaron that Moses was gone for good and that they had better create a new god. So they made the golden calf, a replica of one of Egypt's deities. While they were dancing around their ready-made god, Moses showed up and pitched a holy fit—literally.

But God was even angrier than Moses. He told Moses that he was going to destroy the Israelites and start over with him. I suppose that we would have called the people of that new nation "Mosesites"! But wanting no part of that plan, Moses begged the Lord not to destroy the people. Moses didn't do so on the basis that the people deserved to be saved. Instead, he appealed to the name of the Lord: "O LORD, why should your anger burn against your people, whom you brought out of Egypt with great power and a mighty hand? Why should the Egyptians say, 'It was with evil intent that he brought them out, to kill them in the mountains and to wipe them off the face of the earth'?" (Exodus 32:11–12).

Moses called on God to honor his name! He appealed to God's reputation with the Egyptians as he begged for blessings for the Israelites. Moses knew what was important. Nations will come and go, kingdoms will rise and fall, but the name of the Lord will endure forever! When we offer petitions to God, we need to ensure that we offer ones that will honor God's name and not just ours.

An old Yogi Berra story about a pious batter expresses this principle pretty well. It was the last of the ninth inning; the score was tied. The next batter stepped up to the plate and made the sign of the cross on home plate with his bat. The famous catcher just wiped it off with his glove and said, "Why don't we let God just watch this game?"

4. The Father Will Give You

Jesus offers a final assurance that the God who hears our requests will answer us: "Then the Father will give you whatever you ask in my name" (John 15:16). But as anyone who has received a negative answer from the Lord is aware, we don't always get just what we ask for. He may give us something different and better than what we requested, but any substitutions are benevolent ones. As Jesus assured us, "Which of you, if his son asks for bread, will give him a stone? Or if he asks for a fish, will give him a snake? If you, then, though you are evil, know how to give good gifts to your children, how much more will your Father in heaven give good gifts to those who ask him!" (Matthew 7:9–11).

God, in his sovereignty, knows what will best meet our needs and fit into his divine plan. And he will work his will in ways we might never imagine. Consider the elderly, Christian woman whose nonbelieving neighbor loved to mock her prayers for daily needs. One evening, overhearing her requests to God for some specific items, he rushed to the store and bought those very things. After placing them on her porch, he rang the doorbell and hid in the bushes. When the woman saw the food she had prayed for waiting on her porch, she began to praise God for it.

The atheist sprang from his hiding place to expose her error. "Look here," he stated. "God didn't get you those groceries. I did, and I have the receipt to prove it! What do you think of your God now?"

"Oh my," she exclaimed, "he's even smarter than I imagined. Not only did he get me my groceries, but he made the devil pay the bill!"

In some ways, it's just that simple. Our task is to ask; God's task alone is to answer. And when he does provide for our needs, it is our further joy to give thanks and tell others of his kindness. Our world needs to hear us telling stories of God's faithfulness. We need to be passing on to our children accounts of the "Margarets" we have known and sharing with each other the prayer victories we have experienced. If we do, we will all be even more inclined to follow Christ's simple words. This faithful pledge from the lips of our Savior will move us to seek God for what we need: "You may ask me for anything in my name, and I will do it" (John 14:14).

What are you waiting for? If you need something, go ask your Father!

SECTION FOUR
WORDS OF CAUTION

"This is going to hurt...a lot," the doctor told my wife. "But it's the only way to avoid a Cesarean section." Our first pregnancy was "breach": The baby was upside down in the womb and headed for a dangerous delivery. So our doctor recommended an approach called an external version.

"Basically, it means we turn the baby around from the outside. We mash on the little fellow and convince him to flip over. But it is painful."

I fully expected my wife to refuse—I knew I would have. But she hung in there and agreed to try it. Thankfully, after about an hour of "mashing," our son turned over and was later delivered without a hitch. I asked Cathryn afterwards, "Did it hurt as much as he said it would?"

"More!" she replied. "But I knew it would all be worth it in the end. I'm just glad he warned me."

Warnings, even the frightening or unpleasant ones are always better than terrible surprises. Jesus agreed and didn't want us to wander into Christianity believing that "This won't hurt at all!" Instead he gave us the warning that we needed: *"Following me will be painful."*

His words sound dire, but they are truthful. And they come from one who knows what it feels like to be despised, rejected, and hurt. But knowing the joy that lay ahead, he faced it all and then called us to do the same.

So take a deep breath, because this *is* going to hurt. Just know that, in the end, it will all be worth it.

If the world hates you, keep in mind that it hated me first. If you belonged to the world, it would love you as its own. As it is, you do not belong to the world, but I have chosen you out of the world.... If they persecuted me, they will persecute you also. If they obeyed my teaching, they will obey yours also.

John 15:18–20

10

DON'T BE SHOCKED:
THEY WON'T LIKE YOU!

John William "Bill" King and two of his buddies were known racists and proud of it. As self-proclaimed "white supremacists," they had often made jokes about what they would like to do to the "worthless blacks" who were moving into their town. And on June 7, 1998, their jokes turned into a hate crime that stunned America. The details were unthinkable.

On that hot, summer night in the sleepy, little town of Jasper, Texas, King and his buddies grew tired of just riding around the countryside. They grabbed an unsuspecting, forty-nine-year-old black man, James Byrd, who was walking home from a convenience store. They then took him to a secluded spot where they mocked and beat him. As he begged for his life, they chained him to the back of their pickup truck and dragged him for three miles until he died. James was literally torn to shreds by the gravel road.

The hateful murderers couldn't keep from bragging about what they had done, and soon the law caught up with them. John King was the first of the three to be tried. He was found guilty of murder and sentenced to death. At his sentencing, he was asked if he had anything to say to the family of the innocent man he had so brutally murdered. While the people in the courtroom held their breath, the convicted man turned to face his victim's family. With a sly smirk, he told them that they could perform a certain sex act on him!

Hate is a powerful drug. It breeds the kinds of actions that nightmares are made of. Just when you think you have eradicated it from your society or your heart, it springs up again. Hate is hard to weed out of even the most pious heart. That's because it feeds on our common emotions: fear and envy. When we fear something, our ultimate defense mechanism is hatred. We may think that if we destroy the thing or person we fear, we will be set free from worry. When we envy someone who receives appreciation, hatred is the sour substitute for offering our congratulations. So it's not hard to see how some people hate the rich because they can afford to live in marvelous houses or hate Muslims because their numbers are proliferating.

And just in case you analytical types think that you are immune to hate's frightening grasp, take note. There is no use in trying to reason with hate—it appears out of the blue and sends logic screaming for cover. Hate is not a brain function. It is a gut reaction. It defies logic. As one country singer sings about the woman who stole her man, "I hate her…and I'll think of a good reason later."

When you are the one staring down the barrel of hatred, it can be pretty unsettling as well. Hate's lack of logic or control causes us to feel as if we've driven into a fierce storm that has come up out of nowhere. We don't know whether to pull over and wait for it to pass or to just keep on driving.

Jesus knew that feeling well because he had often faced hatred from the religious leaders of his day. That's why he detoured from the words of comfort and solace that he had been offering to his disciples in order to sound a storm warning. "If the world hates you," he said, "keep in mind that it hated me first. If you belonged to the world, it would love you as its own. As it is, you do not belong to the world, but I have chosen you out of the world. That is why the world hates you" (John 15:18–19).

These words of caution are healthy ones for us to consider. Like some of the early believers, we, too, are surprised when the world doesn't give us the Nobel prize for our kindness. The world often looks right past the work we do with the homeless and demands to know instead why we are antihomosexual. The world pays virtually no attention to the good done by the church in keeping families strong but wants to picket our buildings because we won't support abortion rights for fourteen-year-olds.

Our first reaction is to say, "There's something wrong here!" But our Lord replies, "Get used to it." Let's consider the hard truth that Jesus imparted to his disciples and glean some principles that can help us hold on when the world's hatred blasts us unexpectedly.

CHAPTER 10

"*They* Hated Me!"

It comes as a surprise to some first-time Bible students that not everyone loved Jesus. From the beginning of his ministry, he made enemies among the Jewish leadership. Whether it was the Pharisees who were threatened by his popularity or the Sadducees who worried that his teaching about the afterlife would topple their religious house of cards, Jesus could hardly enter a village without making folks upset. For a fellow whose greatest teaching was "love one another," Jesus sure could tick people off!

Jesus fared little better among the Galileans. Remember the time he drove two thousand demons from a wrecked soul who had been forced to live in a graveyard in chains? Naked and crazy, this possessed man had lived a life of self-mutilation and self-exile in the cemetery for who-knows-how-many years. Along came Jesus, and the man was cured instantly. When the townspeople heard about it, we might expect them to give Jesus the "Good Neighbor Award" or at least thank him for getting rid of a local menace. Not hardly. Mark's Gospel tells us that they "began to plead with Jesus to leave their region" (Mark 5:17). It was a polite way of saying, "Get out of town by sundown!"

The hatred that had followed Jesus to Jerusalem ultimately led to Calvary. When his crucifixion loomed mere hours away, Jesus could have assumed that his disciples would expect the obvious. Surely they would recognize that their fate would not be too different from that of their Master. Yet he felt the need to guide them in thinking along these lines.

"If I came and did God's will," he said, "and they hated and persecuted me, when you come and do God's will, you should expect the world to _____."

The blank should have been easy for the disciples to fill in. And it should be easy for us to fill in as well. Or is it? We, too, can delude ourselves into thinking that things are different. *Our world is more sophisticated and less barbaric than it was in Christ's day,* we think. *Why, just look at the places where hatred for Christianity seems subdued if not altogether overcome.*

Of course, we have plaques on our walls from humanitarian organizations that work with churches to help the needy. We share resources with philanthropic groups that use church connections to help improve our communities. But we sometimes forget what Jesus taught: Any attempt to solve the world's problems without him is doomed to fail. Just try explaining that to your local, atheistic philanthropist and see what kind of a hug you receive.

We must face the fact that Jesus is a polarizing figure. We can't "sort of" accept him. Either we stand with him or we stand in opposition to him. His warning from Matthew 10:32–33 demands it: "Whoever acknowledges me before men, I will also acknowledge him before my Father in heaven. But whoever disowns me before men, I will disown him before my Father in heaven." That kind of "take-it-or-leave-it" lordship is bound to ruffle feathers. "So don't be surprised if the world hates you," Jesus whispers. "Just remember, they hated me first."

But that was just the first reason why the winds of hatred will blow our way. Jesus next shared another key factor.

CHAPTER 10

"*You* Are Not like Them!"

There's an ironic truth in modern-day America: Homosexuals and Christians share a common burden. Both are persecuted for being different. The young woman who commits to remaining a virgin until she is married is teased right along with the openly gay seventh-grader. The husband who refuses to divorce a wife who repeatedly has been unfaithful is called a fool, just like the politician who voluntarily comes out of the closet about his sexual preferences. Actually, in some places, the Christian is more reviled, but the reaction to Christians and those involved in homosexual sin stems from the same phobia. The world is uncomfortable with anyone who is strikingly different. Jesus' words once again prove to be prophetic: "If you belonged to the world, it would love you as its own. As it is, you do not belong to the world…. That is why the world hates you" (John 15:19).

This statement may need to be proved to those who consider the current crop of tongue-piercing, grunge-wearing Generation Xers to be way-out and different. We are certainly living through a generation that is coming of age in loud rebellion. Many younger people want to divorce themselves from society and make their own way. But oddly enough, while they scream, "I'm not like you; I'm different!" they all tend to wear the same clothing, pierce the same body parts, and listen to the same music. Ever look at a group of them hanging out at the local Starbucks or waiting in line at a movie theater?

They all look alike, those rabid individualists.

But rather than giggle at their struggle for identity, let's consider the uphill task they face if they choose to be as truly different as Jesus was.

Christians are called to live lives that are out of this world. In his garden prayer, he said, "I have given them your word and the world has hated them, for they are not of the world any more than I am of the world. My prayer is not that you take them out of the world but that you protect them from the evil one. They are not of the world, even as I am not of it" (John 17:14–16).

Let's admit it, a monastery sounds like a pretty nice option compared to facing the jeers of an unbelieving world. Maybe you, too, have longed to run away to an imaginary Christian haven where everyone bids you Godspeed each morning and gives you a thumbs-up as you drive to church on Sunday. But as appealing as this may sound, our Lord viewed everything differently.

Jesus asked God not to remove us from this world because it needs to see our divinely inspired difference. Nonbelievers need to be exposed to a radical vision of godliness and love that leaves their senses reeling and their minds ajar. To accomplish that, we must be as alien to the secular world as Christ was. We must live out such different lives of compassion and holiness that other people are compelled to ask, "Who are you?" The very fact that we are different gives us the glorious opportunity to tell them why.

Let's consider one more aspect of the hatred Jesus predicted. For even in sharing the good news, He didn't want us to be surprised again when the world still doesn't catch on.

CHAPTER 10

" *T* h e y D i d n ' t U n d e r s t a n d M e ! "

When was the last time someone screamed at you in a foreign language? My wife and I had that unsettling experience on a train in Germany a few years ago. We had been traveling to a family conference in Berchtesgaden, where I was to speak. After the long flight from California, we were taking a five-hour train ride to the conference site. We found an empty compartment and put our feet up on the padded bench seats. After the cramped conditions on the airplane, it felt positively heavenly to stretch our legs. We quickly dozed off.

Suddenly, the compartment door flew open and an irate German man began to chew us out in his native tongue. It took us a minute to wake up enough to realize that this was no nightmare. I had thrown a jacket over my wife and me, and I had to fight it off in order to sit up. This seemed to rankle the stranger even more. As we scrambled to find our stubs, I kept saying, "We have a ticket," but it just seemed to make matters worse. Finally, he shouted one last flurry of what sounded like German expletives, slammed the compartment door, and strode away.

Only after finding our ticket stubs at our destination did we realize that we had been in the wrong section of the train. We never knew for certain, but I suspect that we were sleeping in that poor fellow's seat! But because we didn't speak his language, we thought the guy had just been a crank who liked to bug tired American tourists.

It's not unfair to suggest that the world may feel the same way we did on the train when it is confronted by enthusiastic Christians.

We come running at them spouting theological catch phrases such as "saved by the blood" or "justified by grace," and they have no idea what we mean. Like that poor German man, we think the world doesn't care, so we just say it louder.

Trying to help us sort out this challenge, Jesus explained that some of the world's hatred comes because people simply don't understand who he is. "They will treat you this way," he said, "because of my name, for they do not know the One who sent me" (John 15:21).

When we confront a world of people whose value system has left them totally unprepared to deal with concepts such as right and wrong, we need to expect that their confusion may turn to disgust. Some people of our generation need a dictionary in order to remember (or learn) what sin is. They can no more comprehend holiness than I could understand the screaming German passenger.

So don't be surprised by the world's confusion-induced hatred. Be ready for it, Jesus taught. Expect it. And when it comes, choose not to respond in kind, but learn to respond like him. Therein lies the secret to handling the world's hatred.

We Are to Respond As Jesus Did

Not only will following Jesus win us the hatred he received, but it will also demand the compassion he lived out. Through an ancient proverb, Jesus revealed the way to handle the world's hatred: "No servant is greater than his master" (John 13:16). So when we are abused, we must turn to the example of our Master and respond as he did.

If the hatred of the world has been leading you to respond in kind, if you have found yourself saying, "They should all be blown away," when you hear about people who commit wanton acts of violence or prejudice like the killing in Jasper, Texas, then read this next section reeeeeally slooowly.

Jesus calls on us to respond to the world's hate with love and forgiveness. I know that the world doesn't deserve love and forgiveness, but then, neither do we. Jesus' example motivates us to give grace to those who abuse us and to turn the other cheek toward those who mock us. Remember, after hours on the cross, he still was willing to pray, "Father, forgive them, for they do not know what they are doing" (Luke 23:34).

Jesus gave us all fair warning of this demand. When he finished the beatitudes in his famous Sermon on the Mount, he closed with these words: "Blessed are you when people insult you, persecute you and falsely say all kinds of evil against you because of me. Rejoice and be glad" (Matthew 5:11–12). If you've ever wondered what there is to rejoice about in being the butt of someone else's joke, consider the fact that it is only when we are hated and abused for our faith that we have the chance to truly become like Christ. So if walking in his footsteps is what you pray for, then get ready for abuse and be ready to respond as he did.

So that we can be as practical as possible, let me offer a little three-part checklist for responding to the world's anger in a Christlike manner.

1. *Pray for them.* First, we are to pray for our enemies. Praying for them is one of the best spiritual exercises you'll ever find. It takes

a really Christ-centered heart to ask God to bless those who have hurt us. Yet that is exactly what Jesus told us to do: "I tell you: Love your enemies and pray for those who persecute you" (Matthew 5:44).

Have you ever tried to do this? If not, why not try it now? Think of someone who has wronged you or your family. Be specific. Think of the person's name. Picture the person's face. Now ask God to pour his richest blessings on that person.

Don't just ask God to straighten out that person. And don't pray like the lady who was so tired of her cantankerous husband that she finally told him, "I'm praying that God will take one of us home, and when he answers my prayer, I'm going to live with my sister in Grand Rapids." Instead, really beseech God to give that person all that he or she desires, to bless that person's life and family, and to watch over that person wherever he or she may go. When we pray for those who hate us, we step into the sandals of our Master and are more ready to respond as he does.

2. Love them. We are to love our enemies. The step from praying for someone to loving someone is not huge. When we consistently lift up another person in prayer, we are more likely to view that person as being valuable and lovable. When we begin to recognize that God created that person, sent Jesus to die for that person, and cares about that person every bit as much as he cares about us, loving begins to come more easily.

Again, Jesus is our example. He looked over Jerusalem—the city that would spit in his face—and he bemoaned the fact that he could not simply gather its people into his loving arms. Caring for lost persons, even those who are belligerent and rebellious, is part of walking the path to the cross. Our love is not to be hidden in our hearts. Through actions and deeds, we are to love the people who hate us. Some people may suggest that we are compromising when we extend kindness to people who hate the name of Christ, but nothing is farther from the truth. When we actively love the people who mock our faith, we are following Scripture's command: "If your enemy is hungry, feed him; if he is thirsty, give him something to drink" (Romans 12:20). This kind of active love helps to prepare our hearts for the most difficult yet most Christlike step of all.

3. *Forgive them.* The only path through hatred is the one called "forgiveness." As long as we harbor the resentment that seems so natural to hold against those who hate Jesus, we are forever kept from being like him.

Is there someone whose hatred you need to forgive? Is there someone who has hurt you? Is there someone whom you have rightly longed to be brought to justice? If so, do your heart a favor and forgive that person. Leave the vengeance business to God. Let me tell you the story of one well-known man who did just that.

On February 9, 1960, Adolph Coors III of the famous family beer business was kidnapped and held for ransom. Seven months later, his body was found on a remote hillside. He had been shot to death. Adolph Coors IV, then fifteen years old, lost not only his father but his best friend. For years, the young Coors hated Joseph Corbett, the man who was sentenced to life in prison for the slaying.

Then, in 1975, Adolf Coors IV, known to his friends as Ad, chose to follow Christ. Although he divested himself of his interest in the family beer business, he could not divest himself of the hatred that consumed him. Resentment seethed within him and would not let him go. He prayed to God for help because he realized how his hatred of his father's killer was alienating him from God and other people. The day finally came when Ad Coors had the opportunity to visit the maximum security unit of Colorado's Canon City penitentiary, where Corbett was held.

What would he say? How would he approach this longtime enemy? Coors decided to tell Corbett that he had forgiven him. But when he arrived at the facility, the prisoner callously refused to see him.

Ad Coors was not to be defeated by hatred again. He left a Bible for Corbett in which he had inscribed this message: "I'm here to see you today, and I'm sorry that we could not meet. As a Christian I am summoned by our Lord and Savior, Jesus Christ, to forgive. I do forgive you, and I ask you to forgive me for the hatred I've held in my heart for you."

Years later, Coors confessed, "I have a love for that man that only Jesus Christ could have put in my heart."

While you wait for Christ's return, allow God to grant you that same love toward those who hate you. Then, when he returns, you can meet him with scars of hatred that have been healed by the curative power of divine grace.

If the world hates you, keep in mind that it hated me first. If I had not come and spoken to them, they would not be guilty of sin. Now, however, they have no excuse for their sin. He who hates me hates my Father as well. If I had not done among them what no one else did, they would not be guilty of sin. But now they have seen these miracles, and yet they have hated both me and my Father. But this is to fulfill what is written in their Law: "They hated me without reason."

John 15:18, 22–25

11

DON'T BE FOOLED: THEY WILL TEMPT YOU!

Do you happen to know Betty Boop's biggest hit song?

If you don't know who Betty Boop is, you've lost the contest. Betty Boop, that little cartoon cutie animated by Max Fleischer, was a favorite decades before Batman met the Joker or the Teenage Mutant Ninja Turtles ate their first slices of pizza. She was a black-and-white heartstopper from the 1930s and '40s who wowed the troops during World War I and the folks back home as well.

And her song? It was the unforgettable "I Want to Be Loved by You!" It even included her trademark lyric "Boop-boop-a-doop!"

Her song is still sung by much-less-famous artists. It's one of those American classics that just won't go away. There's a good reason for the song's popularity. Everybody wants to be loved. Love is as normal as breathing. It has been the source of countless songs, plays, and movies because everyone can relate to the desire to have somebody say, "I love you."

But as Jesus continued to warn his close followers during his last night with them, he turned to a darker side of the word *love*. He had already used the word *love* twenty-four times at that famous table. He commanded his friends to "love one another" four times in just the previous few verses. But in John 15:19, his use of *love* stands out as strikingly different.

Here Jesus wasn't talking about the Father's love or the devotion that Christians should show to one another. Here he spoke of a seductive, sinister love that would be waiting for his followers after he left. "If you belonged to the world, it would *love* you as its own," he warned. "As it is, you do not belong to the world, but I have chosen you out of the world. That is why the world hates you." For the first time in this final teaching discourse, Jesus used the word *love* in a negative sense. He wanted the disciples to know that there was another love in town, another suitor looking for someone who wanted affection.

This guy would be smooth. He would offer flowers and candy like they'd never seen before. He would sing sweet songs and make them feel as if they were the only ones. If they would just belong to him, he'd make sure they felt loved and appreciated every day. Today, that same suitor still sings the same, old tune: "I want to be loved by you...."

But don't let him fool you. He really just wants you to become like him. He's the same guy we discussed in the previous chapter who will hate your guts if you stand firm with Christ. Of course, he wants you to know it doesn't have to be like that. "You and I don't have to be on opposite teams," he offers. "Can't we work together?" He is willing to love and accept you as his own if you do just a tiny bit of assimilating into his culture—the world's culture. A little compromise here, a small moral lapse there, and bingo! Why, you fit right in!

The pressure to conform had been tough enough when Christ walked with the disciples. The religious leaders had accused him of everything from winebibbing to treason in order to try to shake up his supporters. But now that he would no longer be by their side to reassure them, the tempting love of the world would be an even greater allure. Paul's warning is appropriate here: "Do not conform any longer to the pattern of this world, but be transformed by the renewing of your mind" (Romans 12:2). Through the ages, the love of the world has become even more tempting. Each new generation of Christians faces this same song: "If you will compromise and conform to our paradigm, we'll let you join the club. We will love you as our own," the world croons. And in our lonely hearts, we hear the haunting strain, "I wanna be loved by you."

Have you felt the tug of the world's come-on recently? Has the pressure to join the club become unbearable during the long, lonely days while you wait for the return of our Lord? Maybe you felt its pull last Friday when you stared at the marquee at the local multiplex: *They say that one is hilarious,* you mused, *but the language is just awful.*

Or was it when you got that invitation to go out for drinks after work: *I know it'll be a blast,* you thought, *but I've heard how this bunch gets when they've had a few.*

Perhaps the tug was strongest when that idea floated across your desk: *This could make us all rich,* you realized. *It's also totally unethical and probably illegal.*

Oh yes, we've all heard the song. We've all gotten the pitch. We've all felt the tug. The world is ready to make a deal whenever we are. We can even keep the fish on our bumper sticker and the cross-shaped earrings as long as we just don't push the issue and become *too* holy.

Sounding as sweet as a Mafia don making you an offer you can't refuse, the world will make it seem so reasonable. "This doesn't have to be hard," they add. "We can both come out of this okay." Soon we're humming right along with them:

"I wanna be loved by you."

But then we come face to face with the words of Jesus. "You are not of this world!" he reminds us, just as certainly as he warned the disciples, that we no longer fit in.

Ever since Jesus pulled the mask off sin, showing it for what it is, there has been no room for compromise. "If I had not come and spoken to them," Jesus said, "they would not be guilty of sin. Now, however, they have no excuse for their sin" (John 15:22). The harsh light of his truth leaves no gray areas. Christ has taken off the table any peace negotiations that don't include complete surrender to him. Détente is not an option. His teaching condemns the very foundations on which this world is built. His lifestyle stands in opposition to the very fabric of this culture. He is like someone from another planet who cannot survive on the tainted air of this world. And when we choose to follow him, we, too, must become resident aliens on this dirt ball. We are destined for a different country, one of our own.

Like Abraham and the nomads who followed him, we are to live as strangers, not settlers. This world is not our home. It can never love and accept us as family while we hold to the truth of Christ. It cannot accept us because it will not accept him. If we wish to hold the hand of the world, we must let go of Jesus' hand. As James put it, "Don't you know that friendship with the world is hatred toward God? Anyone who chooses to be a friend of the world becomes an enemy of God" (James 4:4).

So how do we avoid assimilation into the world's ways? How do we keep from succumbing to the "loving" offer it holds out? Christ told his students that they must be "as shrewd as snakes and as innocent as doves" (Matthew 10:16). So let's obtain some wisdom about how the world seduces us into compromise and assimilation so that we can avoid it.

*G*oing Down:
The Assimilation Escalator

There is something irresistible about escalators. All kids love them. Turn a couple of kids loose on a set of escalators for five minutes, and sooner than later they'll try to run up the down escalator.

It is guaranteed. Scientists have proven that it's an undeniable human urge. There's something within us that says, "Go on. You can do it."

An escalator is a pretty good image for us to keep in mind as we consider the allure of compromise with and conformity to this world. Once we start riding the down escalator, it's hard to stop and change direction. And if we're enjoying the ride, we give little thought to what is waiting at the bottom.

Total assimilation.

Being just like the world.

Immersion in sin.

Denying our Lord and his values.

No Christian I know ever woke up one morning and said, "I think I'll lose my faith this afternoon." It doesn't start like that. It begins with the smooth, easy ride of a down escalator. We're hardly aware that we're moving, but our downward progress is undeniable.

Paul's description of the way in which the nation of Israel managed the trip gives us a pretty good outline of the process. In 1 Corinthians 10:1–5, he wrote, "I do not want you to be ignorant of the fact, brothers, that our forefathers were all under the cloud and that they all passed through the sea. They were all baptized into Moses in the cloud and in the sea. They all ate the same spiritual food and drank the same spiritual drink.... Nevertheless, God was not pleased with most of them."

Israel began as a nation birthed by God. He brought them out of Egyptian bondage by the power of his hand and gave them a new home. Whether it was manna and quail or law and guidance, God provided everything they needed for their survival. What a faith-building experience it must have been to see the Red Sea part or to watch water spew from a rock. Yet despite this amazing beginning, most of the Israelites turned back to the world from which they had been delivered.

How could this have happened? How could people have that kind of supercharged spiritual beginning and then fall away? We could ask the same question of a thousand ministers' kids who no longer darken a church door or a million wayward Christians who grew up saying prayers at every meal but now say "thank God" only when they make it safely past a speed trap. But instead, let's allow Paul to guide us down four of the steps of assimilation that Israel took.

Step 1: Thinking about it. "Now these things occurred as examples to keep us from setting our hearts on evil things as they did" (1 Corinthians 10:6). Notice the key phrase Paul uses, "setting our hearts on evil things." He employed this phrase several times in his letters, but he used it more frequently in a positive sense as in Colossians 3:1: "Set your hearts on things above."

God has given us the ability to set our hearts and minds where we choose. When temptation comes knocking, we have the option to say, as a friend of mine likes to put it, "Excuse me, Jesus. Will you get that?" However, we often like to get a good look at the caller before we send him away. We want to make sure he is who we think he is before we send him packing, so we ponder the offer. We peruse the selection. We're not choosing to sin, mind you, we're just...*thinking about it.*

Although that phrase may sound innocent enough, it holds the seeds of total assimilation into the world's culture. Every sin begins when we are just *thinking about it.*

> The extramarital affair starts
> when we are just *thinking about it.*
> The shocking embezzlement scheme begins
> when we are just *thinking about it.*
> The drug addict begins his tragic slide
> when he is just *thinking about it.*

When we allow our hearts to be set on evil—even for a little while—we have stepped onto the path leading to moral destruction. That's why movies and television are so persuasive. We can watch a lifestyle we would never live. We can enjoy the sin of the week vicariously without dirtying our hands. *It's just a movie,* we think. But the real damage is invisible. Once we start to think about sin, to mull it over in our hearts, we have already moved one step down the escalator.

Please don't confuse setting our hearts on sin with the momentary images that fly uninvited into our minds. A pretty girl strolls by at the beach, and before we can say "thong bikini," guys have sex on the brain. Or an unfriendly motorist cuts us off, and the words we would like to shout back instantly fill our brain. That happens too fast for us to control. The key question is what we do next. Do we roll that thought around in our minds? Do we let it percolate and see where it leads? Or do we boot it out as unsuitable for Christ's person and replace it with something godly? As my father used to say, "You can't keep a bird from landing on your head, but you don't have to let it make a nest there!"

Step 2: Rationalizing it. Paul went on to warn, "Do not be idolaters, as some of them were; as it is written: 'The people sat down to eat and drink and got up to indulge in pagan revelry'" (1 Corinthians 10:7). Once the escalator has taken us to the thought level, our next challenge is to deal with the conflict that evil thoughts create in our hearts. It is clear that evil doesn't fit in well with the surroundings. *Playboy* magazine just doesn't look right on the table next to the Bible. That's where idolatry comes in.

You read it correctly: idolatry. "Do not be idolaters." If it sounds a little out of place, just consider what it means. Idolatry has long been one of God's most hated sins. He included it in the Ten Commandments and punished his people severely for turning to other gods. Why? Because idolatry was a way of *substituting* some other authority or standard for God's.

And guess what? The standards that were substituted were always more lenient and gratifying for the flesh than God's. That's why the Israelites could eat a meal God had provided for them at the foot of Mount Sinai one moment and party around the golden calf the next. If you were to hold a popularity contest for deities, who wouldn't expect Bacchus to win out over Jehovah? Bacchus throws better parties!

It still works the same way today. When we begin to consider an evil action, when we ponder an illicit thought, our conscience chides us. When God says, "That's wrong," we are forced either to reject those offending thoughts or to make provision for their acceptance.

This is where rationalizing comes in so handy. We begin to substitute God's standard for any one of a dozen readily available worldviews.

> If it doesn't hurt anyone else,
> it's not wrong.
> If it's not illegal,
> it's not really wrong.
> If everybody else is doing it,
> it can't be wrong.
> If nobody knows I did it,
> it's not wrong.

The list is endless. Satan has his people working on new possibilities even as you are reading these words. He'll have us redefining "wrong" until it becomes a practical impossibility. With the right situational ethics, any action could be construed as moral.

Did you feel it? We just moved down another step. But hang on, this next one is a doozie.

Step 3: Doing it. Now Paul takes us into deep water. "We should not commit sexual immorality, as some of them did—and in one day twenty-three thousand of them died" (1 Corinthians 10:8).

Until this moment, sin has all been in our heads. We have thought about doing wrong. We have even rationalized why this wrong thing would not be so wrong. But we have not done it…yet. If you have stood at the brink of this abyss recently, you know that it is not as wide a chasm as it first appears. Once we have thought about and visualized an action for a sufficient amount of time, actually doing it comes fairly easily.

I am compelled to pause to note the power of the multimedia that surrounds us. When children see violence and slaughter long enough, are they not more comfortable with the concept? When a young girl watches enough romantic sex outside of marriage, is she not more at ease with the idea? God thinks so. That's why we are encouraged to guard our hearts and our minds in Christ. Otherwise, that which at one time seemed to be an unthinkable leap becomes one small step. So…

> You do it.
> You take it.
> You touch her (or him).
> You lie about it.

When we do, we expect the world to come crashing down around our ears. We are ready for the sirens to go off and the storm troopers to come rushing in. After all, doesn't the "Good Book" say, "You may be sure that your sin will find you out"? (Numbers 32:23). Sometimes it doesn't, and if we are careful, it won't. We make an astounding discovery that sin seems *manageable*. We can do something sinful on Saturday night and take communion on Sunday morning. The wine doesn't burn our lips, and the bread doesn't stick in our throats. So we arrive at a wonderful, awful conclusion: We can get away with it!

See how quickly we have come so far? And we descend the escalator with some august characters. David never imagined becoming an adulterer and a murderer when he noticed how attractive his neighbor's wife was. Peter never dreamed of denying the Lord while he warmed himself by the fire. They just wanted to fit in. They just wanted to have a little fun. They just wanted to get away from their troubles.

If you have found yourself here and think that this is the last stop on the escalator to Hades, I have some bad news for you. Satan isn't done with you yet. What began as a little love affair with this world soon becomes destructive. Once we have crossed over the line to action, we have committed ourselves. We are no longer just pondering, we are doing. In Paul's words, we are offering ourselves as "slaves to sin" (Romans 6:6).

At this point, we have but two choices. We can stop, confess our sin, and start over. Or we can press on and sear our conscience with more excuses, which leads us to the bottom level of our downhill trip.

Step 4: Defending it. Once we've crossed the line, we wonder what comes next, and Paul didn't mince any words. "We should not test the Lord," he wrote. "And do not grumble, as some of them did—and were killed by the destroying angel" (1 Corinthians 10:9–10).

Sure enough, we even begin playing games with God to see if we will get caught. We meet in places that are not quite as safe. We stash our trash in spots where it is just a little less likely to stay hidden. We cover our trail with a little less thoroughness. Will anyone notice? Will people catch on? We are testing God. We want to see what will happen if we bring this fight into the open. And we are not prepared for what comes next.

When the inevitable confrontation takes place, we may be surprised by the spirited defense we offer. "You don't understand!" we protest. "You weren't there! You can't imagine how I felt!"

If these words don't sound familiar to you, they sure do to me. I have sat with many people who have wandered down this escalator, and I've heard phrase after phrase of this stuff. Whether they cheated on their spouses or lied about their taxes, they all sound the same when the whole thing crashes down.

I'm not putting these people down. They've already done that themselves. I do want to show the folly of their defense. The wise man of the ages said, "There is a way that seems right to a man, but in the end it leads to death" (Proverbs 14:12). The defensive statements and the self-absolving logic are all part of the package. When we finally hit the bottom of the escalator, we are fully absorbed into the fabric of the world. We even defend it!

What is the result? The world loves you for it!

You get a divorce:

You finally got some smarts and dumped that jerk!

You lie to get ahead:

What do you know! You're a real person after all.

You have an affair:

Now you're really living, man!

And somewhere in the back of your mind a song plays that you just can't seem to shake: "I wanna be loved by you."

The Path Back Up

A sad-faced crowd gathers around the bottom of the down escalator. Half of them still can't believe where they are. The other half is kicking themselves for ever starting the ride. What is even more amazing is how few of them notice that there is another escalator right next to the one they rode down. But this escalator goes up. Paul described it this way: "God is faithful; he will not let you be tempted beyond what you can bear. But when you are tempted, he will also provide a way out so that you can stand up under it" (1 Corinthians 10:13).

God is faithful, and he plans ahead. Knowing that we would be lured by the love of the world and that we would dabble in its wares, he placed a path back to him right in front of us. Paved with the blood of Christ, it is the way to get home again. Its steps are labeled with words like *repentance, contrition,* and *confession.* The way isn't fancy, and it isn't smooth, but if we will turn our back on the love of this world and choose to live like aliens, we can reclaim our identity and regain our faith. If we will walk away from the seducing crowd and focus on the One who loved us with all his life, the One who gave himself for us, we can find the affirmation and love for which we long.

Jesus knew that you would want to be loved. So he loved you first, best, and strongest. While you wait for your lover's return, don't listen to the *wannabes* who crowd the airwaves. They want you to love them, but they haven't got what he has.

Let John's words help you to stay true! "Do not love the world or anything in the world. If anyone loves the world, the love of the Father is not in him" (1 John 2:15).

A time is coming when anyone who kills you will think he is offering a service to God. They will do such things because they have not known the Father or me. I have told you this, so that when the time comes you will remember that I warned you. I did not tell you this at first because I was with you.

John 16:2–4

12

WHEN THEY HURT YOU, DON'T LET GO!

The images I saw on the screen simply couldn't be real. I struggled to believe that this kind of thing actually went on in our "tolerant," modern world. Surely no one treated other people this way simply because of their "religious persuasion."

Having received my share of e-mails about terrible persecutions of Christians overseas that proved to be unsubstantiated or in some cases manufactured, I had come by my skepticism honestly. But these scenes were on a screen right in front of me, and the guy who had filmed them was standing right beside me.

Produced by a group called The Voice of the Martyrs, the video had been shot by my friend's production company. I had to ask him, "Is this stuff real?"

He nodded solemnly as we watched a child of ten or twelve bound by ankle chains being beaten across his back with a stick. Another was being forced to copy verses from the Koran while overseers struck the heads of any children who moved too slowly. All the while, an announcer recounted horror stories of beatings and mutilations suffered by Christians who lived in this radical, Muslim country.

Persecution at the dawn of the year 2000 didn't make sense to me. I thought that feeding Christians to the lions went out with wearing togas. *Surely these guys had read the Global Agreement on Human Rights,* I mused. But despite our world's seemingly progressive sensibilities and New-Age tolerance, people are still doing what Jesus warned they would do. They are hurting Christians simply because they are Christians.

Admittedly, most of us have never seen the kind of harsh persecutions described in the New Testament. But whether it is done with a stone or with a sneer, persecution will come to every follower of Christ. So we would do well to ponder the last warning Jesus offered during his final meal with his disciples.

A Final Warning

The apostles had seen Jesus being mocked and taunted by the religious elite of their day, but now they needed to be prepared for what was about to happen to their Lord—and later to themselves. Christ didn't want the onslaught of hatred and violence to sweep away their faith, so he pulled back the curtain of the future a little farther and gave them a picture of the days ahead. "All this I have told you so that you will not go astray," he said. "They will put you out of the synagogue; in fact, a time is coming when anyone who kills you will think he is offering a service to God" (John 16:1–2).

This warning was among the last things Christ told the disciples in the upper room. And he probably saved it for last for a good reason. His warning certainly included tough words to hear: persecution, pain, problems. They were fearsome enough to motivate most of the disciples to go back to the fishing boats. But they needed to hear those words, and so do we.

Although the violence that the early Christians faced befalls few in our culture, every believer must be prepared to face the pressure of persecution. As one newly baptized believer complained to me, "I thought when you became a Christian everything in your life got better." Someone had failed to warn this new believer about Satan's never-ending campaign to beat down the faith of every Christian and to beat back the kingdom of Christ.

But the middle of a battle is no place to discover that the other side is willing to hit hard. This was a lesson I learned the hard way on the football field. My father always wanted me to be a sportsman. He had done well in sports and dreamed of his son following in those footsteps. So he made sure I tried one season of each of the major sports: baseball, basketball, and football.

I started with baseball and quickly proved that I lacked the coordination and speed to succeed. Basketball was more of the same. My skinny frame was not up to the demands of hustling up and down the court, and my determination was weaker than my frame. By the time football season began, I was getting tired and my father was getting desperate. If I failed at football, the only letter I would have on my jacket would be from the chess club.

So on a pretty autumn afternoon, Dad came to watch my first flag football game. Practice had been uneventful, with most of our time dedicated to throwing and catching. In the process, I finally found something I was pretty good at: hiking the ball. I became the starting center.

Our team lost the toss, and I sat watching our defense do its best. Thanks to a quick interception by our fellows, our offensive team was called to the field only three minutes into the game. In the huddle, I listened intently for the only thing that mattered to me: the number for the hike. It was "twenty-one." I had practiced for weeks snapping the ball only when the secret number was called. I had honed my aim until I was able to lodge the football right in the quarterback's hands ten out of ten times.

The only thing I hadn't thought about was the other team. Someone should have warned me. As soon as "twenty-one" was called and I snapped the ball, I got knocked hard right on my rear! I felt like I had been hit by a dump truck and found myself staring up at a huge kid who just laughed at me. The quarterback's throw was incomplete, but I paid no attention. I was focused on my aching rear and the sadistic punk who had knocked me down.

I went back to the huddle in a fog and within seconds was back on the line to hike. I glanced up at the kid I had mentally named "Tank." He was digging in his knuckles and preparing to charge. The quarterback yelled the sequence, and I shot him the ball just before I got slammed into the grass again. My teeth rattled; my behind ached. Without thinking, I said to a still-smiling Tank, "What are you doing?"

"Knocking you on your butt! And I hope you like it, 'cause I'm gonna do it all day long."

And he did.

Do you know what made me most angry? Nobody had warned me. No coach had told me that while I minded my own business just trying to hike the ball, there would be a kid whose whole goal in life was to make my rear throb! It wasn't right. Someone should have told me to expect opposition.

That's exactly what Jesus did. He warned us that there would be another team on the field and that its members would be playing for keeps. They would do their best to distract and dispirit us. And if they couldn't do that, they would just try to knock us down. In fact, we can say that persecution is the devil's team trying to knock us down enough times to knock us out of the game.

Thankfully, Jesus didn't leave us unprepared. He made sure that we were well aware of the opposition and their strategy. Just in case the peaceful setting we enjoy most of the time has lulled us into thinking that the other team is finally giving up, let's consider the truth about persecution and the plan our Lord has for us to overcome it.

Three Truths about Persecution

As is true of most aspects of the Christian faith, the reality of persecution has been interpreted in various ways. Some people view the lack of active persecution in our country as a sign of lethargy in the American church. Others claim that the relative peace we enjoy is a gift from God that may only last a short time. What is the truth? Let's consider what Jesus said.

1. *The absence of persecution is no proof of God's blessing.* Through the cycles of history, the cause of Christ has moved in and out of favor. Some governments have called Jesus the "savior" while others have considered his words to be the "opiate of the masses."

Simply because some Christians live in a persecution-free zone does not prove that God is pleased with their government or their church. The Old Testament record shows that Israel most often wandered away from God when times were good. Their wickedness was the result of believing that if nothing bad was happening, they must be doing something right. A wealthy drug dealer or a rich pimp could make the same statement.

Moreover, godly people who have faced persecution would argue against this logic as well. A no more immoral government could be imagined than the one that existed in Rome in A.D. 90 when Christians were burned at the stake and fed to the lions. Yet the church of that time was peopled with great men and women of faith who certainly had the Lord's approval. Thankfully, no Roman Christian leader suggested that God was punishing them through the persecutions. Rather, they took heart in Paul's words to Timothy: "In fact, everyone who wants to live a godly life in Christ Jesus will be persecuted" (2 Timothy 3:12).

Indeed, Paul's words should give us pause when we consider the relatively low level of persecution we face in this "Christian" country. Never should we assume that our government's willingness to let us worship as we please is a sign of God's approval of our government or our churches. Our leaders are just as godless as any who came before them, and our faith is often as weak as our leaders' morals.

The freedom and peace that we enjoy should prompt us to be thankful, not prideful. We are not free from fear because we are so good or because our country is so noble. As with all things temporal, freedom and peace will pass. The future of the world may well bring more trying times for Christ's church. Yet whether leaders support Christ or abhor him, the calling of the church to be faithful remains the same.

2. The presence of persecution is no guarantee of God's approval. Too many believers want to count present persecution as proof of their purity. "We must be doing something right," they say. "Look at how much opposition there is!" Whole movements have been founded on this principle, which is sometimes called the "bunker mentality." This belief stems from the notion that there are only a few true believers left and anyone who truly stands up for what is right will face grievous trials.

Cult leaders love this kind of thinking because it feeds into their followers' isolation and leads to a complete distrust and dismissal of all criticism. It grants the leaders immunity from all who would point out their mistakes and makes them impervious to even the most justified and rational critics.

But this belief is evident on a much smaller, less ominous scale as well. Teenagers may find encouragement to pursue extreme tastes by their parents' harsh reaction to those very choices. New Christians sometimes assume they are under spiritual attack when a non-believer simply asks them to give reasons for their newfound faith. Members of a church who want to change an aspect of the worship or tradition sometimes claim that they are on God's side simply because others rudely oppose them.

In each of these cases, the nasty attitude of the opposition is viewed as confirmation of one's own uprightness. When the enemy is the bad guys, we must be the good guys! Right?

Wrong! Bad guys fight bad guys every day. Just because I am being shot at by the Indians doesn't mean I'm John Wayne. I may just be a horse thief! In fact, more often than not, my selfishness and other faults have earned me my wounds. When I am criticized for being rude or uncaring in my expression of my faith, it is probably just criticism, not unwarranted persecution.

Moreover, the possibility exists that the persecution I face may be coming from God. When the Lord struck down Paul on the road to Damascus, the future apostle wasn't so steeled in his anti-Christian resolve that he called it a "demonic attack." Instead, he recognized it as God's correcting hand and was humbly obedient. We, too, must keep our eyes open. We must beware of the temptation to use the presence or absence of persecution as a guarantee of anything.

3. Our reaction to persecution is a sign of our faith. When Jesus warned his disciples of coming persecution, he did so purposefully. He wanted them to be prepared to respond properly. And therein lies the real battle, for the goal of persecution is not to discredit the persecuted people but to discredit the faith for which they stand.

Satan wants not only to stop us from speaking out for Christ but to prove to the watching world that we are no different than unbelievers and that our Lord is no different from their gods.

We can, of course, give in to persecution by responding in kind. Like the holy warriors of ancient times, we can find ourselves using the enemy's tactics without realizing it. We can start mocking the atheist and insulting the agnostic. We can turn our anger on the Satan worshiper instead of on Satan. When we do, we dishonor not only ourselves but our King.

That's why Jesus' warning is so important. He wanted his followers to respond to persecution in a manner that would certify the reality of their faith to their persecutors. As he looked into the disciples' faces in the upper room, he knew that they would become prisoners and martyrs on his account. Whatever their fate, he wanted them to face persecution with a strength and depth of commitment that would be a testimony to the truth of his words—and the power behind them.

How did he want them to respond to the coming persecution? He knew that some of them would want to pick up a sword and retaliate, as Peter would in the garden. He knew that others would run and hide, hoping to escape the embarrassment and pain. But he made it clear that if they fought or fled, they would fail. So he prepared them to respond in a divinely inhuman way to those who would hurt them. His method should come as no surprise to us. It was the way he had both modeled and taught: "Love your enemies, do good to those who hate you, bless those who curse you, pray for those who mistreat you" (Luke 6:27–28).

CHAPTER 12

Overcoming our natural tendency to hurt those who hurt us is a monumental task. It can be accomplished only with the aid of the Holy Spirit and a deep devotion to Christ. But the task must be accomplished, because the important question is not whether we are hurt but what we do when it happens. Persecution will come and go. Our response to persecution is what interests Christ most. The Irish preacher Jim McGuiggan told a story that illustrates this principle well.

A hard-nosed British staff sergeant was whipping his new recruits into line when he learned that one was a self-professed Christian. He noticed that the young man never used any of the foul language that was constantly heard in the barracks and that he prayed every night before retiring. The agnostic sergeant was determined to beat this sign of weakness out of the young soldier. So he began giving the recruit the most distasteful and difficult duties. He rode the young man hard as he worked, waiting for his Christian facade to break. Yet the young man never wavered.

After one particularly grueling day of marching through muddy marshes until every man was sore and sullen, the sergeant led his troops back to their barracks well after dark. As they collapsed onto their bunks exhausted and broken, he watched in amazement as the young Christian recruit knelt by his bed to pray before he would give himself much-needed rest. In a moment of anger and frustration, the sergeant yanked off one of his muddy boots and hurled it the length of the barracks at the young soldier. It narrowly missed him, and he kept on praying. Consumed by hate, the sergeant threw his second boot and hit the young man squarely in the head. Silence fell in the barracks as the young soldier slowly rose from the floor, a small stream of blood coursing down his cheek from a gash over his eye. The sergeant stood smiling, ready for the fight he had longed for, but his young opponent simply knelt back down and silently finished his prayer. Defeated, the sergeant stormed into his room, slamming the door.

The next morning, feeling worn out and depressed from the previous night's contest, the sergeant opened his door. There, just outside, were his boots, cleaned and polished to a gleaming shine by the young Christian soldier.

Three Principles for Facing Persecution

If that story leaves your knees weak, don't feel bad. A compassionate response to persecution is not a habit that is easily developed. But Christ offered three fundamental principles that can set us on the path of learning to handle persecution as he did.

1. Learn to discover the blessing in persecution. Loggers in the Pacific Northwest know where to find trees whose wood has the finest grain and is the best for woodworking. They don't find them in the valleys, where they are shielded from the storms. The best trees grow high up on the mountainsides. From the time these trees were small, they were beaten by strong winds that toughened them and gave them their fine, beautiful grain. Without the stress of howling winds, trees never develop their inner strength.

So it is with us. The pressures of persecution can strengthen our souls and develop our spirits. Jesus told us as much in the Sermon on the Mount when he said, "Blessed are you when people insult you, persecute you and falsely say all kinds of evil against you because of me" (Matthew 5:11). Persecution could never be viewed as a blessing unless God were able to use it to produce something good in our lives.

No rational person seeks persecution or prays for problems, but personal growth seems to come only through the refiner's fire. That is why James restated the truths of Jesus: "Consider it pure joy, my brothers, whenever you face trials of many kinds, because you know that the testing of your faith develops perseverance" (James 1:2–3). Our faith development flows from our trials. As one friend of mine puts it, "The Lord gives us friends to push us to our potential—and enemies to push us beyond it."

Knowing that strength of faith and character are born during hard times, we can begin to view persecution in a new light. Rather than running from it, we can choose to grow as a result of it. By standing fast in the face of jeers or jokes, we can learn to trust in the One who faced more persecution than we will ever know. And with each angry jab or unjust slur, we come one step closer to what the heavenly maker wants us to become.

2. Recognize the power of persecution. If we are to maintain our faith in the face of opposition, we need to recognize the enemy's strategy. Through persecution, Satan hopes to capture our attention and entice us to focus our energy on ourselves. Persecution can attack three levels of self:

Self-Esteem
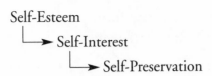
    └──► Self-Interest
          └──► Self-Preservation

The first level of persecution attacks our *self-esteem* and is an attempt to cause us to become embarrassed or uptight about our faith. When we're under attack at this level of persecution, we start to worry that if we mention Jesus at work or place a Bible on our desks someone will think less of us. We become oversensitive to the slightest reference to religion. We become afraid to say anything about Christ or the church for fear that our words will mar our reputation or strain a friendship. By attacking our self-esteem, Satan is simply trying to get us self-focused.

If he fails at this level, Satan will often press on to the next level: *self-interest.* At this point, we no longer worry about our reputation alone, we fear for our job or our position. An atheistic manager or hostile boss may press us about working on Sundays or joining coworkers for a drink at the bar after work. We fear that to refuse might jeopardize the promotion we're hoping for or, worse, set us on a course toward dismissal. We realize that our commitment to honesty may threaten our employers' "big deals." We each know that if we tell the truth, a client may walk away and our future with our company may depart with him or her.

Make no mistake, persecution at this level is real. Christian men and women face this kind of quiet persecution every day, and many of them succumb to the pressure without realizing what has happened.

Finally, Satan's ultimate persecution focuses on *self-preservation.* Thankfully, this is a level most Christians will never face, yet it's one for which everyone must be prepared. At this level, the pressure is obvious, the cost is high, and our very bodies are the targets. And there are no boundaries or borders that will protect us. It doesn't matter whether it happens in Beijing, China, where a Christian church is raided and attendees are carted off to jail, or in Laguna Beach, California, where a young Christian man was beaten because he called homosexuality a sin. When the powers of darkness take the battle to this stage, believers can only trust in their Lord and stay faithful to his cause.

If you consider each of the levels of persecution we have addressed—self-esteem, self-interest, self-preservation—the common denominator is clear: *self.* The effectiveness of persecution lies in getting us to focus on ourselves. Knowing this, we can also see that the power to defeat persecution lies in keeping the focus where it belongs—on our Lord and his example.

3. Allow persecution to point you to Jesus. Ironically, the same persecution that can distract us from Jesus can serve to point us back to him if we know how to face it. Consider the vision of Hebrews 12. The writer paints a sports scene from a track-and-field course. He imagines the Christian running in a kind of hurdle race in which scorn, shame, weariness, and sin are the obstacles to be overcome. As the runner sets out on the course, he seems to hurdle every obstacle with grace and ease. What's his secret? Look at his eyes, and you will know.

The key to winning this race is not how high one jumps but where one looks. The runner of Hebrews has his gaze fixed not on the obstacles but on his Savior: "Let us fix our eyes on Jesus, the author and perfecter of our faith, who for the joy set before him endured the cross, scorning its shame, and sat down at the right hand of the throne of God" (Hebrews 12:2).

When the persecutor tries to direct our vision toward the mirror or toward the pains ahead, it is more important than ever for us to look to the Lord. The One who warned us that hard times would come also said that the world hated him first (John 15:18). He did not direct us to go where he had not already walked. When our sides ache with the sting of mockery, he reminds us that he was there too. When our hearts break in the trenches of pain, his serene face can provide a guiding light.

It all depends on where we fix our gaze.

During World War I, a British soldier lost heart for the battle and deserted. Trying to reach the coast and catch a boat to England, he ended up wandering through a moonless night, hopelessly lost. In the darkness, he came across what he thought was a signpost. It was so dark that he began to climb the post so that he could read it. As he reached the top, he struck a match so that he could see and found himself looking squarely into the face of Jesus Christ! Rather than climbing a signpost, he had climbed a roadside crucifix. At that moment, he remembered the One who had died for him, the One who had endured persecution and never turned back. The next morning, the soldier was back in the trenches.

When we face harsh persecution and the opposition seems overwhelming, all we need to do is strike a match in the spiritual darkness and look on the face of Jesus Christ. If we fix our gaze on his example, if we focus on his patient grace, if we listen to him say, "Father, forgive them, for they do not know what they are doing" (Luke 23:34), then we will gain the power to respond with his strength and grace.

In a little while you will see me no more,

and then after a little while you will see me.

John 16:16

CLEARING THE TABLE: "I'LL SEE YOU AGAIN"

The conversation was finished. All the things they needed to know until his return had been said. Had they listened? Would they understand? Only time would tell. And time was the one thing he had run out of.

Soon the soldiers would confront them.

Soon the betrayer would kiss him.

Soon the little dinner party would be scattered to the four winds and the trials would begin. And it would all end on a hill not far from the table where they had eaten the Passover lamb together.

He would not leave them without hope. "I am coming back. We will be together again," he promised. But in the long years of waiting, those words would grow dim and dusty, like an old fairy tale or a faded family photo. The disciples would wonder and doubt. They would silently review the promises and wordlessly ask the question: "Will he come back? Has he remembered me? Does God care?"

Those questions still dance on the lips of believers. We have the precious words he left us. We have the Spirit's invisible guarantee. We have one another to cling to when the going gets rough. But in the end, each one must answer those questions for his or her own heart.

When the last hours of life creep slowly away,

When the mate we have trusted betrays us and runs,

When the child we love dies tragically young—

Then how can we be sure of his promise,

of his return, of his love?

Maybe the only way is to see it through heaven's eyes. If you are willing, then this analogy of mine might help you. Ready? Imagine this:

Turning on your radio on a drive home one evening, you just catch the end of a story about a strange disease outbreak in a remote part of India. It's a flu-like illness, but it is much more toxic than the normal strain. A few villagers have actually died from it, and the Center for Disease Control is sending over a team of doctors to investigate. That ends the report, and you don't think much about it as you pull into your driveway. A new disease, that's all.

But the next Sunday, coming home from church, you hear the same story again—only this time the report says that over three hundred villagers in the back hills of India have died in the last month from this weird disease. At the dinner table, one of your kids mentions hearing about it in science class, and that night CNN runs a brief spot on their Headline News, calling it the "Mystery Flu." Details are still sketchy, they say, but this could become a serious problem for India.

Twenty-four hours later, their predictions are proved more than right: It's not just a serious problem for India; it's hit Pakistan, Afghanistan, Iran, Malaysia—you name it. The evening news anchor breathlessly recounts the rapid spread of the disease through almost every country near India and suggests that it was all being kept out of the news for political and economic reasons. Our president is shown making a statement at a press conference, saying that he and his family are praying and hoping that a cure will be found quickly. But the president of France goes a good deal farther: He shocks all of Europe the next morning by closing the borders of his country to flights from India, Pakistan, or anywhere else where this disease has been reported.

But the action was too late. That very evening CNN rebroadcasts a clip from a French news program of a weeping woman fleeing a Paris hospital. Her words are translated into English: "There's a man in there dying of the mystery flu." It has come to Europe. Panic strikes. Fatalities are reported in Italy, Spain, and England; and the numbers rocket daily. The disease itself becomes the center of a worldwide scientific study. Experts from around the globe are examining the virus, and the Internet is choked with new sites carrying information. As best the scientists can tell, the disease is passed through the air. You can be infected with it for a week and not know it. Then come four days of unbelievable symptoms followed by death.

By the weekend no one is surprised when the president of the United States makes the following announcement: "Due to a national security risk, all flights to and from Europe and Asia have been canceled. If your loved ones are overseas, I'm sorry. They cannot come back until we find a cure for this terrible disease."

The nation reacts in fear. Street corner vendors start selling surgical masks at double the price, and doomsday preachers point to the Bible and call the disease "a scourge of God." And you find yourself asking quietly, "Is it?" Then at a Wednesday evening church prayer meeting, somebody runs in from the parking lot and says, "Turn on a radio, turn on a radio." The minister sticks a microphone to a little transistor radio so the whole church can hear the terrible news: "Our on-site reporters have confirmed it: Two dock workers are lying in a Long Island hospital dying from the mystery flu." Within what seems like only hours, the thing just sweeps across the country. Similar reports come in from California, Oregon, Arizona, Delaware, Georgia, and Florida. All the while scientists and doctors work around the clock trying to find an antidote. All hope seems lost, and all you can do is pray.

And you do—like you never have before.

Then all at once the news comes out. The viral code has been broken. A cure can be found. A vaccine can be made. But it requires a certain blood type from someone who hasn't been infected, someone who's blood is pure. The Emergency Broadcasting System begins to alert all citizens in areas where the Mystery Flu has not yet reached: "Please, go to your local hospital and have your blood tested. When you hear the sirens sound in your neighborhood, please make your way quickly but safely to the closest hospitals."

When the sirens sound on your block late on Friday night, you and your family follow the line of cars to the local hospital only to get in another long line with the rest of your neighbors. They've set up a makeshift admitting station in the parking lot, and a crew of nurses and doctors are pricking fingers, taking blood, labeling the samples, and shuttling them back into a large white van, where a mobile lab has been setup. They quickly take blood samples from your family and then instruct you to wait in the parking lot. "If we call your name," one tired-looking doctor shouts through a megaphone, "you can be dismissed and go home. Either your blood is already infected or you don't have the blood type needed."

You stand around with the rest of your stunned and scared neighbors, wondering what the world has come to in just ten days. You wonder if the answer is "the end of humanity." When suddenly a young man in a lab coat comes running out of the mobile lab screaming. He's yelling a name and waving a clipboard. "I can't understand what he's saying," an older lady next to you says. The man yells it again, and your son tugs on your jacket and says, "Daddy, that's my name."

Before you can move, two doctors have grabbed your boy and are hustling him toward the lab. "Wait a minute, hold it!" you protest. Another doctor grabs your arm and says, "It's okay, his blood is clean. His blood is pure. We want to make sure he doesn't have the disease. We think—we hope he has the right blood type."

Five tense minutes later, doctors and nurses come pouring out, crying and hugging one another—some are even laughing. It's the first time you have seen anybody laugh in a week, and an older doctor walks up to you and says, "Thank you, sir. Your son's blood type is perfect. It's uninfected, and we can make the vaccine. We can save the world." As the word begins to spread across the crowded parking lot, people start praying and laughing and crying.

But then one gray-haired doctor pulls you and your spouse aside and says, "May I see you for a moment? We didn't realize that the donor would be a minor and we need…well, we need you to sign a consent form." He hands you a pen and clip board, but as you scan the form you notice that the number of pints of blood to be taken is left blank.

"H-h-how much blood will you take?"

That's when the old doctor's smile fades and he says, "We had no idea it would be a small child. We weren't prepared for this. We will need it all. I'm sorry."

"But…but…" you protest. "Won't you give him a transfusion? Won't you replace the blood? If you just drain him he will—"

"You don't understand. If we already had his blood type we wouldn't need his. I'm truly sorry, but we are talking about saving the whole world. Please, sign the form."

And in a numbed silence, you do. Then they ask, "Would you like to have a moment with him before we begin?" They lead you to surgical suite in the hospital, and through a window you see your son sitting on an examination table, looking like the frightened little boy he is.

Could you walk into that room as he says, "Daddy? Mommy? What's going on?"

Could you take his hands and say, "Son, we love you, and we would never ever let anything happen to you that didn't just have to be. Do you understand that?"

Could you leave when the doctor pokes in his head and says, "I'm sorry, we've...we've got to get started. People all over the world are waiting."

Could you walk out while your son says, "Dad? Mom? Why...why have you forsaken me?"

I couldn't. But God did.

Any Father who loves you enough to give his only son's blood to make you clean has earned all the trust we can offer. Any Savior who would give his life's blood for our mistakes has earned all the allegiance we can pledge. His promises are faithful. His word is solid. His love is proved by the blood stains on that hill outside Jerusalem. And when we question any of the things he so wanted us to have confidence in, we need only to remember what he paid for our salvation to be renewed in our faith. Oh, he will return. And may we all trust in his words and be ready to meet him when he comes.

Even now, come Lord Jesus!

STUDY AND DISCUSSION GUIDE

Introduction. Setting the Table

1. Read John 13:31–38. Noting the questions that the disciples asked Jesus when he announced his departure, what three questions would you have asked? How do you think Jesus would have answered them?

2. When Peter asks to go with Jesus, what does he proclaim himself willing to do? Why do you think he added that claim?

3. Read John 18:15–27. Peter's claim of faithfulness was proved false at the courtyard fire. Sometimes we claim stronger faith than we actually possess. What kinds of settings cause you to make such claims? What kinds of settings make it the most difficult for you to stand up for your faith?

Chapter 1. Don't Be Afraid

1. Read John 14:1–4. A troubled heart can become a way of life. What symptoms show that a Christian is choosing to live in fear? Which of those do you see in your life right now?

Fear Has Always Been Connected to Sin

2. Genesis 3:1–10 tells the story of the first sin. Because of guilt and sin, Adam and Eve hid from God in the bushes. How do we hide from God today? How effective are our hiding places?

3. What thoughts do you think were going through Adam and Eve's heads while they hid from God in the garden? When do those thoughts run through your head?

4. Satan began the whole mess in the garden by lying to Adam and Eve. When we fall into sin, what lies do guilt and shame tell us to keep us in hiding?

The Power of Fear Is a Matter of Focus

5. Imagine that fear holds the binoculars of your heart. Where does fear want to point your vision?

6. When we look in the direction fear prescribes, what part of the picture aren't we seeing? What is fear trying to hide from our vision?

Conquering Fear Is a Matter of Choice

7. Read Luke 12:4–5. What is the difference in being scared of God and having a proper "fear of the Lord"? Is it ever right for a Christian to be scared of the Lord?

8. Proverbs 1:7 tells us that the fear of the Lord is the beginning of knowledge. Why is it just the beginning? What would be the "end" of knowledge? How does this compare with the way we train children?

9. The three great motivating forces in our world are fear, reward, and love. How does God use them to motivate his children?

10. What advise would you give a Christian friend who said, "I have always been a fearful person. I can't change that"? How does one take back control of one's heart's binoculars?

Chapter 2. Don't Stop Trusting

1. Read John 14:5–13. Thomas is often called "Doubting Thomas." What clues does his question at the table give us about how he looked at life? In what ways are you prone to think like Thomas?

2. How does Jesus' use of the word "know" in verses 6 and 7 differ from Thomas's use of the word in verse 5? What can we learn from this?

3. Some say that a person can never really know that God exists or that Jesus is real. My grandmother would say, "You just know it deep down in your knower." How would you respond to someone who said that no one can be completely sure of Christ's claims?

Who Did Jesus Claim to Be?

4. Read John 8:24; 14:6. How are the claims of Jesus exclusive? What about those who suggest that there are many roads to heaven?

What Did Jesus Do to Prove His Claims?

5. Thomas got to touch Jesus' side, but in the years that followed, do you think he still struggled with doubt? Would you have still struggled? Could seeing a miracle totally erase all doubt forever?

When Has Jesus Let Us Down?

6. In Luke 6:47–48, Jesus describes the lives of people who trust his words. How does this word picture help us defend the trustworthiness of Christ's teachings? What story would you tell from your own life to show that Jesus' words are faithful? (You may wish to write it down and share it with a friend.)

Where Else Could We Turn?

7. There are many theories unbelievers offer for how Jesus' tomb wound up empty. Which of the alternative explanations for Christ's resurrection is the most plausible to you? What are the logical

problems that exist with this view? What questions would you ask someone who believed it?

Why Not Trust Jesus?

8. Read John 6:67–69. When people turn away from the promises of Jesus because they do not trust his claims, to what do they turn? What other claims are they then choosing to believe? How might this perspective help when sharing with a nonbeliever?

9. Which of the five questions from the chapter—Who? What? When? Where? or Why?—is most helpful for your faith-walk? What other questions would you add to the list?

10. Read Hebrews 11:6. Knowing how important trust and faith in God are, what could you do today to help strengthen your faith?

Chapter 3. You Are Not Alone

1. Read John 14:15–31. Jesus promised that he would not leave us as orphans. When do you most feel like a spiritual orphan? How should the presence of the Holy Spirit impact those feelings?

2. Jesus refers to the Holy Spirit as a counselor. How does this name describe the function of the spirit in the Christian's life?

3. Jesus also calls the Holy Spirit the "Spirit of Truth." What does this indicate about the Holy Spirit? How would this title help the person who fears what the Holy Spirit might do?

The Reality of the Holy Spirit

4. Read John 14:17. How would you describe the presence of the Holy Spirit to a non-Christian? What analogies or metaphors would you use to describe his invisible presence?

5. How has the Holy Spirit made his reality most evident to you? Write down your testimony and be ready to share it with a friend.

The Role of the Holy Spirit

6. Which of the titles Jesus uses for the Holy Spirit best describes your relationship with him? Why? Which title do you hope your relationship develops toward?

7. Paul's picture of the struggle between body, mind, and the Spirit in Romans 7 shows those three powers at work within us. How can Christians weaken the body while strengthening the Spirit?

8. If the mind can overrule the body, what can you do to make your mind more sensitive to the Spirit's directions? How can the logical side of our mind come into conflict with the Spirit? When do you face this most often, and how do you deal with it?

The Results of the Holy Spirit's Presence

9. From reading John 14:27, what is a key symptom of the Holy Spirit's presence in the believer's life? How evident is this in your life? What choices could you make to bring even more peace into your life?

10. Through the Spirit, Christ is present with believers all over the planet. That also means he is with us every minute of every day. How should that truth impact our speech? Our actions? Our relationships?

Chapter 4. Stay Close to Me

1. Read John 15:1–8. When Jesus warns the disciples that they should remain in him, he implies that this might not be easy. What are the forces that pull us away from the hand of Jesus? When have you found these forces pulling you the hardest?

2. Read Philippians 3:18–19. Some of the pressure to let go of Christ's hand comes from outside the believer, but other pressures are really coming from within. What are those inner pressures? Which are the hardest for you to resist? Why?

Remain in Me Because I Am the True Vine

3. Consider the story of the Israelites and the golden calf (Exodus 32:1–8). What prompted Israel to abandon the true God for an idol? Which of those same motivations are at work in you today, pulling you away from Christ?

4. Look at the lists of "false vines" on page 62. List three others that could be included on this list. Which one is the toughest for you to ignore? Why is it the most difficult for you? Pause right now and pray that God will give you strength and discernment to avoid that false vine.

5. How can religion itself become a false vine that sways us from Jesus? How can one identify and protect against that sort of religion?

Remain in Me Because My Father Is the Gardener

6. How does the image of God as the gardener make you feel about your Christian life? What security does it provide? What concerns? If God is the gardener, what kind of plant would you be? Why?

7. Jesus says the gardener both prunes and cuts off branches. How has God been "pruning" in your life? What things is he wanting to "snip off" just now that are inhibiting your being more fruitful?

Remain in Me Because You Can't Bear Fruit Alone

8. Jesus made it clear that we can't bear fruit without him. In what ways do you find yourself trying to "bear fruit" without Jesus' help? When does this most often happen, and what can you do to avoid it?

9. Unattached branches are doomed to wither. If a Christian friend said, "I'm worried that I may be a cut-off branch." How would you help him or her find peace? What questions would be important in determining if he or she was attached to the Christ, the true Vine?

Remain in Me Because If You Do I'll Make You Fruitful!

10. Read 1 Corinthians 3:6–7. If it is God through Christ who makes us fruitful, why need we worry about bearing good fruit at all? What is our part in the process?

Chapter 5. Get Along

1. Read John 15:9–17. Jesus commanded that we love one another. Some say that love cannot be commanded or controlled. How would you respond to that? If we are commanded to love, what does that tell us about the nature of love?

2. Read John 17:20–21. Why do you think that Christians often fight and disagree so violently with one another? How does this impact the world's view of Christ's church?

Jesus' Love Comes from Another World

3. How much does God love Christ? What adjectives would you use to describe that love? Knowing Jesus loved us with that kind of love, how does that make you feel about your value and relationship to Christ?

4. On earth, our love is metered by time and circumstances. God's love is divine and complete. If God knows all of our imperfections and faults, how can he love us so completely?

5. Jesus uses the love that parents have for their children to teach us about his love for us. What memory from your childhood best defines the love your parents had for you? If you are a parent, what has that experience taught you about God's love?

Jesus Loves with a Savior's Love

6. When Jesus washed the disciples' feet in John 13:1–17, the Bible says he was showing them "the full extent of his love." How could this action have been more loving than going to the cross? What made the foot-washing so important?

7. When Jesus washed Peter's feet, Peter protested. What would your reaction have been? Why?

8. How would you present a picture of Jesus' washing of Judas's feet? If you put a cartoon "thought bubble" over each head in the picture, what would you put as Judas's thoughts? What would you put as Jesus' thoughts?

Jesus Wants Us to Share His Love

9. Read John 3:16. We cannot give a love we have never received. What keeps you from fully believing and experiencing the depths of God's love for you? When in your life have you felt that love the deepest?

10. Write a letter to yourself from God. In it, express in words just how much God loves you. When you have finished, read it aloud to yourself and then give thanks to God for his love.

Chapter 6. Do As You're Told

1. Some say that *obey* is a dirty word. How would you respond to that? What makes obedience a negative concept for many?

2. Read John 15:10–11. Jesus linked joy with obedience. What experience in your Christian life best confirms this connection? How has that event impacted your faith in Christ's commands?

The Nature of Joy

3. In John 17:13, Jesus teaches that his words are the path to the "full measure of [his] joy." Yet some see Christians as dour, unhappy people. Why do these stereotypes exist? What prompts modern believers to be less than joyful?

4. Paul warned one church that it seemed that something had taken their joy (Galatians 4:15). List five things that most often rob

you of joy? Which of them are connected to some form of disobedience? Which is the toughest for you to fight?

The Needs of Sin

5. Would you agree with C. S.Lewis's description of sin: "A gray day in a British midland city"? How does sin pretend to be exciting and romantic? How can Christians learn to see through this mask?

6. In Romans 6, Paul warned that sin wants to become our master. Can you take part in a sin without becoming enslaved to it? How can you tell when a sin has made you its slave?

7. Identify an experience in your life when a sin fooled you into thinking it was exciting but ended up being slavery and pain. What one sentence could you write on a note card and read whenever you are tempted to help you remember that event?

The Power of Obedience

8. Read Hebrews 5:8. Do you think Jesus ever disobeyed his parents? Why is it significant for us to know that Jesus learned to obey? How can this help us in our struggles with sin?

9. When do you find it easiest to choose to obey Jesus' commands? Is there anything in those moments that can help you when tougher times come?

10. The chapter ends with a story of a boy falling in love. How do the voluntary choices we make when in love relate to our obedience to God? If God is someone you are "in love with," what does he want from you right now instead of candy or flowers? How could you give him that right now?

Chapter 7. You've Got a Friend

1. Read John 15:13–15. List the names of your six closest friends. What do they all share in common? Add Jesus' name to the

list. Does his name seem out of place? How? What does he share in common with your other friends?

2. Jesus called his disciples friends, but some Christians are uncomfortable with such a familiar term. What do you think prompts that discomfort? How can the concept of friendship with Jesus be misunderstood or abused?

3. The picture of Jesus as our defense attorney is a popular one. What kind of confidence should that inspire in Christians? How can we keep that thought before us through each day?

Friendship Is Born out of Freedom

4. Some parents refuse to take their children to church because they want them to freely choose their own faith. How do you feel about that decision? In what sense do we freely choose our faith, and in what sense is it inherited? When do you think faith truly becomes our own.

Friendship Is Built through Communication

5. Prayer is the way we share our hearts with Christ. What kinds of things do you pray most about? Are these the things that are most often on your heart? What are three things you can do to make your prayer conversations with Christ deeper?

6. If a friend said, "My prayer life feels lifeless and flat," what advice would you give him or her? How could the concept of friendship with Christ help?

Friendship Is Based on Sacrifice

7. Read John 15:13. Is there a friend to whom you would donate an organ? If asked to do so, what would be your criteria for deciding?

8. Write a letter to Christ asking for the donation of his heart. What reasons would you give? What promises would you make?

Friendship Is Preserved through Accountability

9. Read Romans 5:8. If God gave us grace freely, how should we extend Christian friendship to others? What if a Christian friend is doing something you consider to be sin? When, if ever, should a Christian friendship be cut off?

10. Respond to this statement: "When I ignore a brother's sin, I am helping him to sin." What about Christ's admonition not to judge others? When does accountability become judgment?

Chapter 8. You've Been Chosen

1. Think of a time you were chosen for some honor. What words described the way you felt at the time? How does that compare with the feeling you have when you consider that Christ freely selected you as his friend?

2. Read John 15:15–16. Though Christ clearly chose the apostles, we are not selected in quite the same manner. Does this mean that we are not chosen by Jesus? In what sense are we chosen?

God's Sovereign Choice

3. List seven names for God used in the Bible. How do they describe God's power and authority? What sense do they give of his jurisdiction and area of control?

4. Read Ecclesiastes 7:14. It has been suggested that no hurtful event on earth can be blamed on God. What does the Bible say about that notion? How can one reconcile the pain and suffering in the world with an almighty and all-loving God?

5. Read Romans 13:1–2. God chose leaders throughout the Bible: Moses, David, Paul, and Peter. Does he still choose leaders today? Does this mean that the leaders we have are good ones? Does this mean that the American Revolution was an act of rebellion against God?

Our Free Choice

6. If God has the ability to choose leaders and control events, why are we taught to choose him? (Joshua 24:14–15). Is there anyway to avoid the consequences of our spiritual choices? If not, who is to blame?

7. James Dobson is quoted on page 133 as saying, "God gave us a free choice because there is no significance to love that knows no alternative." Why is it important that we know sin is always an available option? How does this explain the presence of Satan in the Garden of Eden?

8. Do you believe Christians ever get to the point where they no longer struggle with making right choices? If one did get to that point, would the gift of free will be lost and would obedience no longer be a choice?

Living with Both Choices

9. Read 1 Corinthians 12:14–18. What does this text indicate about God's choice in placing each Christian in the body? If we are chosen with a purpose, how should that impact the way we set our priorities? How should that affect the way we view other Christians?

10. In Luke 22, two chosen apostles make poor choices. Peter and Judas both deny Christ. What leads one to destruction and the other to repentance? Did Judas have a choice? What can we do to follow Peter's path and not Judas's?

Chapter 9. If You Need It, Just Ask

1. Read John 14:13–14; 15:16. List the top five reasons you believe Christians don't pray more often. Which of those reasons apply to you?

2. Many go through cycles in their prayer life. When is your

prayer life the strongest? What do you learn from that answer? When is your prayer life the weakest? What do you learn from that answer?

If You Ask

3. If God can read our thoughts, why is it important that we verbalize our needs in prayer? What does faithfulness in prayer do for other aspects of our Christian life?

4. Read James 4:1–3. What are wrong motives for making requests in prayer? As God's children, don't we have the right to ask for anything we want? How can one gauge the requests that are being made to see if they are out of wrong motives?

Whatever You Ask

5. Are the requests you make in prayer typically too large or too small? How does the story of Abraham's boldness in asking God for mercy on Sodom impact your answer? How significant is the fact that Abraham was not asking for something for himself?

6. Can a Christian ask God to do something outside the "laws of nature"? What examples can you find in Scripture of God granting or denying these kinds of requests?

In My Name

7. When you conclude a prayer "in Jesus' name," what are you really saying? How might it impact your requests if you started the prayer with that phrase?

8. By asking in Jesus' name, we are suggesting that the requests are in keeping with Jesus' nature. How should that awareness color our prayers? Can one ask for something good that is not in keeping with Jesus' nature? How can you avoid that mistake?

9. Read the story of Moses' saving Israel from God's wrath in Exodus 32:7–14. Did Moses actually change God's mind? What was

the motivation behind his request? How did that impact the answer he received? How can we apply this prin-ciple to our prayer life?

The Father Will Give You

10. List five specific prayer requests you have made in the last year and write down the answers you received. How many were "Yes"? Can you see any blessings in the times God answered "No"? Take a moment and give thanks for both.

Chapter 10. Don't Be Shocked: They Won't Like You!

1. What is your definition of a "hate crime"? Does the crucifixion of Jesus fit that description? Why?

2. Read John 15:18–19. Jesus told us we would be hated. Have you ever experienced prejudice based on your faith? What did the experience do to your tolerance of others?

"They Hated Me!"

3. Why did some people hate Jesus? Do you think this was an exception to the rule or the norm? If Jesus was hated by most people, how do you explain his triumphal entry into Jerusalem?

4. Jesus' authority and uncompromising attitude prompted some to attack him. Do you ever feel angry or frustrated about Jesus? How would you respond to the statement, "If the words of Jesus aren't making you mad every now and then, you just aren't listening"?

"You Are Not like Them!"

5. If Jesus made people angry, should his church be doing the same thing today? How can we bring people to Christ and make them angry at the same time?

6. Read John 17:14–16. Jesus prayed that Christians would be different from the world. For those who see you outside your home

and away from church, list five significant things that would make you stand out as a believer. Are their some items missing from that list that you know should be there? What are they?

"They Didn't Understand Me!"

7. Many non-Christians find that believers speak in "coded language." We use religious jargon to describe our faith. How can we avoid being incomprehensible to the world? What steps can you take to be clear in the way you share Christ?

8. Imagine that you are riding in an airplane with someone who has never heard the story of Jesus. How would you tell them the gospel? What key elements of the story would they need to understand?

We Are to Respond As Jesus Did

9. The chapter ends with a three-step approach to responding to hatred like Christ (pages 164–167). What are the three steps? Which is most difficult for you?

10. List three people against whom you hold a grudge or who may consider you an enemy. Take time right now to ask God to bless them and forgive them their wrongs. If they are not Christians, is this a futile prayer?

Chapter 11. Don't Be Fooled: They Will Tempt You!

1. It is natural to want to be loved. How does this natural desire become a temptation for the Christian? What would you recommend that new believers be told about this?

2. Read Romans 12:1–2. Peer pressure is a key element for social formation. The Christian is encouraged to resist it. Can we encourage positive peer pressure without also empowering negative peer pressure?

3. When does the pressure to conform to the world most affect you? When do you feel the most safe? What proactive steps can you take from what you see in those answers?

Going Down: The Assimilation Elevator

4. Read 1 Corinthians 10:1–5. How would you describe the level of blessings and "god involvement" Israel was enjoying in this passage? What would you expect about the depth of their faith at that point? Is the "nevertheless" of verse 5 surprising? Why?

5. Chapter 11 of this book identifies four steps from the verses that follow. List the four steps in order. What is the significance of the first step? What makes it so powerful?

6. Rationalizing is compared to idolatry. How is it like substituting an idol for God? In what areas of your life have you substituted another standard for Christ's? Why do you think it happened? What actions would be required to recommit to Christ's standards.

7. Read Matthew 5:17–30. Is Jesus saying that thinking about sin is just as bad as doing it? If so, what would you say to the person who said, "If I've thought about it, I may as well do it!"

8. When a Christian chooses to sin, the first defense he must make of his actions is to God. Think about the last time you deliberately chose to sin. How would you defend that action to God? To your Christian friends? On what would you base that defense? How does that answer help you see the reason you may have chosen to sin?

The Path Back Up

9. To change our direction, we must first recognize the areas in which we are moving. Name three areas where you see yourself moving down the Assimilation Escalator. What can you do about those areas in which you are just now at the "Thinking About It" level?

What about the "Rationalizing It" phase? What about "Doing It" and "Defending It?"

10. On page 182 there are some possible names for the steps that lead back up. Put these in what you believe would be the correct order and add to them. What would be the very first step back up? What would be the last step? Where would asking for forgiveness fit in the order? Where are you right now in your life?

Chapter 12. When They Hurt You, Don't Let Go!

A Final Warning

1. What form of persecution have you seen or experienced? Do you believe persecution has been increasing or decreasing in our world? What leads you to that conclusion? What do you believe we should expect in the next fifty years?

2. Read 2 Timothy 3:12. Is this Bible prediction still true? How would you teach this promise to a new Christian?

Three Truths about Persecution

3. How would you respond to someone who suggested that the lack of persecution in America is a sign of God's blessings? Is the Bill of Rights a blessing from God? Is the right to worship without government intervention a right given by God or man?

4. How can just criticism be mistaken for persecution? What is the difference between the two? Which do you experience more of?

5. Read Matthew 26:50–52. What does Peter's action tell you about his response to persecution? Is it ever right to defend yourself against unjust persecution? How does Jesus' instruction on "turning the other cheek" factor into this setting?

Three Principles for Facing Persecution

6. Read Matthew 5:11. What is the blessing Jesus was referring to that comes from persecution? How can we give thanks for that blessing and at the same time ask God not to bring persecution on his people?

7. In Acts 4:24–30, when the first Christians were persecuted, for what did they pray? What can you learn from this?

8. On page 197 is a chart showing three levels of persecution. Each of them contains the word *self.* What is the significance in that, and how can it help you stand up under persecution? Which levels have you experienced recently? How did you handle it?

9. Respond to this statement: "If only the church were more persecuted, she would be more strong." Is persecution a prerequisite to growth? Should Christians be praying for persecution? What about the opportunities for evangelism that a lack of persecution provides?

10. Hebrews 12:2 advises the struggling believer that he should focus his eyes on whom? How can the mental image painted in that text help us to stand firm under persecution?

Epilogue. Clearing the Table: "I'll See You Again"

1. Review all twelve of the truths Jesus wants every believer to know. List the three that you most need to affirm in your life? Which is the most important right now?

2. As you consider the gift God gave when he sacrificed Jesus for our salvation, what confidence does it give you about Christ's return? How does it help you to stay committed to the things he wants every believer to do?

3. Make a list of practical steps you can take this week to keep

the twelve principles from the Last Supper teaching of Jesus before you every day. How could you share them with another Christian friend in a nonthreatening and creative way? Pray that God will give you the opportunity to do that now.

Look for these other books from Howard Publishing

Daring to Dance with God–Jeff Walling
Timeless Moments–Alton Howard
The Heartlifters™ Series
The Hugs™ Series
The Hugs from Heaven™ Series
Circle of Friends–Point of Grace
Sometimes Miracles Hide–Bruce Carroll
Nighttime Is Just Daytime with Your Eyes Closed–Mark Lowry
Piper's Night Before Christmas–Mark Lowry
My Mother's Favorite Song–John William Smith
My Mother Played the Piano–John William Smith
The God of the Towel–Jim McGuiggan
Jesus, Hero of Thy Soul–Jim McGuiggan
Where the Spirit of the Lord Is...–Jim McGuiggan
Opening Windows–Max Lucado and others
The Names of Jesus–Rubel Shelly
What Would Jesus Do Today?–Mike Cope & Rubel Shelly
Churches That Heal–Doug Murren
Fantastic Families–Dr. Nick Stinnett and Joe Beam
Becoming One–Joe Beam
Becoming One Workbook: Exercises in Intimacy–Joe Beam
Forgiven Forever–Joe Beam
Seeing the Unseen–Joe Beam
Too Close to the Flame–Dr. Gregg Jantz
Broken and Battered–Muriel Kanoza
Will I Ever Be Whole Again?–Sandra P. Aldrich
What Kids Wish Parents Knew about Parenting–Joe White

Audio and video tape teaching resources
are available from Jeff Walling's Western Christian Ministries.
Visit their Web site (www.WCMstuff.com).